The NetWare 386 Manual Maker

The NetWare 386 Manual Maker

CHRISTINE MILLIGAN

The Complete Kit for Creating Customized NetWare 386 Manuals

M&T BOOKS

M&T Books
A Division of M&T Publishing, Inc.
501 Galveston Drive
Redwood City, CA 94063

Limits of Liability and Disclaimer of Warranty
The Author and Publisher of this book have used their best efforts in preparing this book and the programs contained in it. These efforts include the development, research, and testing of the theories and programs to determine their effectiveness.

The Author and Publisher make no warranty of any kind, expressed or implied, with regard to these programs or the documentation contained in this book. The Author and Publisher shall not be liable in any event for incidental or consequential damages in connection with, or arising out of, the furnishing, performance, or use of these programs.

Library of Congress Cataloging in Publication Data

Milligan, Christine
     The NetWare 386 Manual Maker: the complete kit for creating customized NetWare 386 manuals / Christine Milligan

ISBN 1-55851-120-2 (book/disk)
1. NetWare (Computer operating system) 2. Electronic data processing documentation I. title

QA76.76.063M563   1990
005.7'1369--dc20

                                      90-22916
                                          CIP

93 92 91 90   4   3   2   1

Editor: Tova F. Fliegel   **Cover Design**: Lauren Smith Designs
Layout: Linda Magyary

Contents

CHAPTER 5: WORKING WITH DIRECTORIES AND FILES (MENU UTILITIES VERSION)

Preface

The idea for this book was born while I was writing the *NetWare386 User's Guide*. As I wrote, I noticed that the text was filled with "ifs." Most of them went something like, "If your supervisor has...then you will...."

The number of qualifications bothered me. I found myself asking questions about users' real needs. I felt that users needed something more specific, something tailored to their installation, but I couldn't write a custom NetWare user guide for every site.

One day, while I was debating these points, the Manual Maker idea popped into my head. I sat at my keyboard, entranced. Such a simple idea, but it solved so many problems! Sure I didn't know if the users at a site needed to know about PCONSOLE; but their supervisor would. And no, I couldn't write a manual tailored to a specific site's requirements; but a supervisor could. So why not give supervisors the raw materials for a manual on diskette, and let them create the manuals?

The more I thought about it, the better it got. If a site had novice, intermediate, and advanced users, a different version of the manual could be produced for each; if the network setup changed, the manual could be revised; if a supervisor had set up a neat little batch file, the batch file could be explained right in the manual. Utilities a user didn't need to know about could be deleted; third-party utilities could be added. The possibilities went on and on. And the manual itself would be easy and cheap to produce: Just print it out on a laser printer, photocopy double-sided pages, punch holes and insert into a three-ring binder, then distribute.

The idea was too good not to act on. So I called Brenda McLaughlin, my contact at M&T. She responded to the idea enthusiastically. The rest of the folks at M&T

Books were just as enthusiastic, and added some innovations of their own (including the "Manual Maker" name.) Together, we developed the idea and hammered out the details. What you're holding in your hands is the result. We hope you'll like it.

Christine Milligan
Provo, Utah
September, 1990

Acknowledgements

Thanks to all the people whose help made *The 286 and 386 Manual Makers* possible:

Dennis and Susan Fredette, for testing the manuscript to be sure a manual could indeed be made from it

Rick Baker, tech editor extraordinaire of *The 286 Manual Maker*

Marj Hermansen, for a speedy, thorough edit of an early manuscript

Tova Fliegel, for patience and grace under pressure

Ed Liebing, for letting me use his network

Novell, Inc., for loaning me software

Most of all, thanks to my husband Steve for his constant support of this and other projects

Why The NetWare 386 Manual Maker is for You

If you need to write documentation or train users, *The NetWare 386 Manual Maker* is for you! It consists of generic end-user documentation which can easily be modified to suit your network setup, your administration philosophy, and users' expertise. Just delete the material you don't want; modify the fill-in-the-blank templates; and add any material specific to your installation. You'll have clear, concise, customized documentation in a matter of days instead of months.

System supervisors can create user-specific documentation. It's easy to delete utilities you don't want users to know about; document how your network is set up; and explain the specific menus, login scripts, and batch files you use on your network.

Dealers and consultants can create custom end-user documentation for their customers, then keep a copy on file for their own use. If the network setup or the customers' needs change, modifying the documentation accordingly is a snap. (Just think what this could do to increase your sales and decrease your support burden!)

End-users benefit from documentation and training that is precisely tailored to their needs. No more searching through pages and pages of irrelevant information, or scrawling notes in margins. The Manual Maker eliminates all of that. Users get a small manual which contains exactly the information they need to be productive on the network immediately.

No matter who you are, *The NetWare 386 Manual Maker* can save you time, money, and frustration. It's an invaluable tool that will pay for itself in a matter of hours.

How to Use The NetWare 386 Manual Maker

Instructions for Supervisors

This chapter provides an overall explanation of how to use *The NetWare 386 Manual Maker*. It also explains some details you should understand before you begin working with the Manual Maker.

Purposes of the Manual Maker

The NetWare 386 Manual Maker has several purposes.

Creates customized user manuals.   The main purpose of the Manual Maker is to help you create user manuals that are tailored to your network setup, philosophy of administering the network, and users' expertise.

The Manual Maker consists mainly of boilerplate documents that you can modify to create your user manuals. Hard copy of the boilerplates forms the bulk of this book; soft copy is provided on the diskettes that accompany this book. The Manual Maker also contains information that helps you to modify the boilerplate text, teach users, and set up their network environments.

Helps you teach users.   You can use the Manual Maker to create training materials or develop course outlines. Because of this, the Manual Maker contains some ideas for teaching and training users in a classroom setting.

Gives tips and tricks.   Many times, what you teach users depends on how you have set up the network environment they work in. The Manual Maker also provides miscellaneous tips and tricks on setting up the network environments.

The Manual Maker Format

The Manual Maker consists of two types of text:

Boilerplate text. This is the actual text that you can modify and include in your customized user manuals.

Ideas and information. This text is intended only for you as supervisor, and is not intended to be included in your user manuals.

The ideas and information intended only for you as supervisor are presented in three forms:

Overall instructions. This chapter and Chapter 8 provide general instructions for using the Manual Maker. Soft copy of these two chapters is NOT provided on diskette, since you would not want to include them in your user manuals.

Divider and preface pages. These are found at the beginning of each chapter. They tell you what file contains the soft copy for the chapter and provide an overview of the chapter. These also give general ideas on how to modify the chapter. Soft copy of divider and preface pages is NOT provided on diskette because, again, you would not want to include them in your user manuals.

Comments. These are scattered throughout the boilerplate text in both the hard and the soft copy. They are boxed to set them apart, like this:

> This is a comment.

The actual form that Comments take in the soft copy depends on what version (WordPerfect or ASCII) of the Manual Maker you are using, as you will see later. Naturally, you won't include Comments in your user manuals.

Backing Up the Master Files

The very first thing you should do with the Manual Maker is to backup the master diskettes and store them in a safe place; this is very important! Backing up doesn't take long, and it can save you a lot of grief. Take a few minutes and do it now.

Now that you've backed up the master diskettes, take a few minutes to skim through the rest of this chapter.

What You Can Create with the Manual Maker

The basics of using the Manual Maker are simple: retrieve the soft copy boilerplate files and modify them to suit your needs. Once the files are modified, you have several options:

Create hard copy user manuals. Print your files, then duplicate, bind, and distribute the manuals as desired. This is a good choice if you have users who are new to computers and are not yet comfortable with working on-line. It is also a good choice if you don't have lots of users and the information in your manuals won't change often. But if you have a large number of users and the information in your manuals becomes outdated rapidly, you may want to consider one of the following choices.

Create an on-line manual. Put the files on your file server and flag them "Read-only" so they can't be changed. Then decide how you want users to access the on-line manual and set it up accordingly. For example, if you want users to access the on-line manual from a menu, add an option to the menu (for example, "Manual") and tell users how to use that option.

Create on-line help. You can import the raw ASCII text from your modified files into an on-line Help facility so users can query the manual. This will be a lot of work, but it may be worth it if you have a lot of users to train.

Using the Manual Maker: A Suggested Approach

I recommend that you work with the Manual Maker as follows:

First, make some preliminary decisions.

1. **Get an overview.** Scan the divider pages, preface pages, and actual text to get an overview of the material contained in the Manual Maker.

2. **Decide on different versions.** Decide if you want to create different versions of manuals for different users. Then, for each version of the manual that you want to create, complete the following steps.

3. **Choose a basic approach.** The Manual Maker is very flexible; the manuals you make with it can be as specific or as general as you want. The more specific you are, the more useful the manual is for your users. But this approach has some disadvantages, too. If you are very specific—for example, if you tell users their exact rights in certain directories—you will probably have to create different versions of the manual for different users. Also, your manuals may become outdated quickly if you change your network setup often.

4. **Copy and rename master files.** Make copies of the master files and rename the copies to avoid accidentally overwriting the masters. If you are creating more than one manual, use extensions to identify which manual the files will be used to create. For example, suppose you wanted to create a manual for beginning users and one for advanced users. You could name the files for the beginning users with a .BEG extension, and the files for the advanced users with a .ADV extension.

Now, start creating the manual(s).

5. **Retrieve and modify soft copy.** Retrieve the soft copy file for the first chapter you want to include in your manual. Then modify the text to suit your needs, using the information contained in the divider pages, preface pages, and comments as guidelines.

   If you plan to include most of the text, just delete the material that you don't want; if you plan to delete most of the text, block copy the first chunk of material you want to include. Then switch to a second document (ALT-F3 for WordPerfect users), and retrieve the material into that document (Press ENTER for WordPerfect users). Save the second document and continue the process until you've copied all the material you want.

   Now go to the next chapter you want to include in your manual, and repeat step 5. Continue until you have modified all the chapters you want to include in your user manual.

6. **Complete your formatting.** Turn to Chapter 8, "Instructions for Final Formatting," for instructions on how to finish your manual.

These are the basics. But before you begin, you should know a little more about the version of the Manual Maker files you are using (WordPerfect or ASCII).

WordPerfect and ASCII Formats

The Manual Maker boilerplate files are provided in two formats, WordPerfect and ASCII. Which you use is a matter of personal preference. I recommend you use the WordPerfect format if at all possible, because then most of your formatting has been done for you; if you use the ASCII version, you'll have to do almost all of your own formatting.

For more information on formatting details, go to the appropriate section:

WordPerfect users—Continue with "Information for WordPerfect Users" on the next page.

ASCII users—Skip to "Information for ASCII Users," beginning on page 15.

Information for WordPerfect Users

The more familiar you are with WordPerfect, the easier it will be for you to use the WordPerfect version of the Manual Maker. I have included instructions for everything you need to know.

The boilerplate hard copy contained in this book is very similar to the WordPerfect boilerplate files contained on the "WordPerfect" diskette that accompanies this book. However, there are some formatting details you need to be aware of.

Page size. The WordPerfect boilerplate files produce standard 10-point text on a standard 8.5 X 11 inch page with wide margins.

Comments. The boxed Comments shown on the screen will NOT print because they have been created with the WordPerfect Comments feature. The Comments you see in this book simulate those you will see on screen, however, you may note some minor discrepancies between the two.

The WordPerfect Comments feature lets you create text "windows" that don't take up vertical lines on the screen or print like regular text. Because of this, Comments provide a handy way to insert explanations, asides, questions, etc., into ordinary text—without having to delete these notes later. I used Comments to put notes in the boilerplate text for you, the supervisor, so that you wouldn't have to worry about deleting those notes from your user manuals.

Comments can be turned on and off. In the boilerplate files that accompany this book, the Comments are turned on so you can see them as you modify the soft copy. But if you want to see how the pages look without the Comments—or how the pages print for your user manuals—just turn the Comments off (more on this later).

I also had to tweak the text to make the pagination in the soft copy files correspond to the pagination in the hard copy of the book. That is why most of the page breaks in the soft copy are hard page breaks. If you turn the Comments off, you may notice some blank and half-blank pages where the Comments were. The best way to handle this is to ignore any awkward page breaks until you have completed your manuals. Then turn the Comments off, page through the document, and delete any unnecessary hard page breaks (see Chapter 8, "Instructions for Final Formatting").

Sequential Chapters and Page References. Chapter numbers, page numbers, and references are fine for conventional books, but I wasn't far into the Manual Maker before I realized they wouldn't work here. Why? Because I have no idea how you will modify the boilerplate text. My Chapter 6 may be your Chapter 3; your page numbers will almost certainly be different.

I tried to work around this problem in the following ways.

First, I kept the overall structure of the Manual Maker simple. For example, all the headings are at one level, because I don't know what you'll leave in or take out. In addition, when there was a choice between repeating material or cross-referencing, I usually repeated material. For this reason, you'll notice quite a bit of redundancy (the repetition of the rights table throughout Chapters 6 and 7 is a good example). If it bothers you, just delete the text you don't want.

Second, I did number the chapters and include some page references. However, chapter numbers are included in Comments so they won't print in your finished text. You can put chapter numbers in the manuals you create if you want to, of course. Just convert the desired Comments to regular text (position the cursor after the Comment, press CTRL-F5, choose Comment, choose Convert to Text). Then correct the numbering if necessary.

All page references have been created with the WordPerfect Cross-Reference feature. I used this feature to mark a reference and a target page for that reference. This allows accurate page references to be generated automatically. The page references you see in the hard copy and the initial on-line files are accurate for the generic Manual Maker before it is modified. After you create your own manuals, you must regenerate these page references. This should be the very last thing you do. See Chapter 8, "Instructions for Final Formatting," for the actual steps.

Loosely Formatted Pages. Wherever possible, I divided the material in the Manual Maker up into small chunks of a page or less, titled the chunk, and started it on a new page. The Manual Maker material is not densely formatted; there are many pages with lots of white space. When you make your user manuals, you'll find that the pages condense quite a bit.

I formatted the material loosely for a couple of reasons. First, I wanted the Manual Maker to be easy to leaf through, both on-line and in the hard copy. I didn't want to make you search for headings in the middle of pages, or scroll through extraneous text on the screen to find something at the bottom of a page. Instead, I designed the Manual Maker so you can use Page Down (the Pg Dn key) and Go To (the CTRL-HOME keys) to "flip" to a page and see its title immediately.

Second, different computers and printers format pages differently. Because of this, a full page may be expanded slightly and become several pages, throwing pagination off.

Because the material is so loosely formatted, you may find yourself with blank and half-blank pages in the manuals you create. I suggest you handle this problem as follows. While you're creating the manual, just ignore any awkward page breaks. Then, after you finish modifying the manual, use the Search (F2) key to find the hard page breaks, and delete those you don't want (see Chapter 8, "Instructions for Final Formatting").

You can format your manuals as densely as you want; but I suggest that you keep one topic to a page where feasible. Manuals that chunk material this way and begin each topic on a new page are easier to use.

Information for ASCII Users

The ASCII files are included for your use if you prefer not to use WordPerfect. They can be imported into the text editor or word processor of your choice. If you choose to use the ASCII files, you'll have to do almost all of your own formatting, since the ASCII text doesn't contain any formatting codes.

In addition to doing your own formatting, you'll also need to be aware of the following details.

Notes to Supervisors. The Manual Maker boilerplate text is sprinkled liberally with notes to supervisors. In the hard copy, these notes can be identified by the boxes that surround them. In the ASCII text, these notes are labeled with COMMENT BEGIN at the beginning of the comment, and COMMENT END immediately following the comment. These codes are included so that you can easily identify the notes and delete them after you have completed your manuals (see Chapter 8, "Instructions for Final Formatting"). You can delete the notes manually, of course; but if macros are available in your text editor or word processor, it's much easier to use them. Your macro should look something like this:

Find COMMENT BEGIN
Move to beginning of the word "COMMENT"
Turn Block on
Find COMMENT END
Delete Block

Sequential Chapters and Page References. Normally, books have chapter numbers, page numbers, and references that depend on a sequential structure. This is fine for conventional books, but I wasn't far into the Manual Maker before I realized it wouldn't work here. Why? Because I have no idea how you will modify the boilerplate text. My Chapter 6 may be your Chapter 3; your page numbers will almost certainly be different.

I tried to work around this problem in the following ways.

First of all, I tried to keep the overall structure of the Manual Maker simple. For example, all the headings are at the same level, because I don't know what you'll leave in or take out. In addition, when there was a choice between repeating material or cross-referencing, I usually repeated material. For this reason, you'll notice quite a bit of redundancy (the repetition of the Rights Table throughout Chapters 6 and 7 is a good example). If the redundancy bothers you, just delete the text you don't want.

Second, I did number the chapters and include some page references. However, all of these references are included in the notes to supervisors. So when you delete the notes to supervisors, the references will also be deleted. You can leave these references in, of course; just make sure you haven't deleted the text that the reference cites, and be sure to change numerical references if necessary.

Loosely Formatted Pages. Wherever possible, I divided the material in the Manual Maker up into small chunks of a page or less, and started each chunk on a new page. The Manual Maker material isn't densely formatted; you'll notice many pages with lots of white space. When you make your user manuals, you'll find that the pages condense quite a bit.

I formatted the material loosely for a couple of reasons. First, I wanted the Manual Maker to be easy to leaf through, both on-line and in the hard copy. I didn't want to make you search for headings in the middle of pages, or scroll through extraneous text on the screen to find something at the bottom of a page. Instead, I designed the Manual Maker so you can "flip" to a page on-line and see its title immediately.

Secondly, different computers and printers format pages differently. Because of this, a full page may be expanded slightly and become several pages, throwing pagination off.

Because the material is so loosely formatted, you may find yourself with blank and half-blank pages in the manuals you create. I suggest you handle this problem as follows. While you're creating the manual, just ignore any awkward page breaks. Then, when you are finished modifying the manual, use your word processor's Search key to find the hard page breaks, and delete those you don't want. (See Chapter 8, "Instructions for Final Formatting.")

You can format your manuals as densely as you want; but I suggest that you keep one topic to a page where feasible. (Manuals that chunk material this way and begin each topic on a new page are easier to use.)

Introduction to Networking and NetWare

The text for this boilerplate chapter is found in
INTRO.WP (WordPerfect version)
INTRO.ASC (ASCII version)

1

Introduction to Networking and NetWare

This chapter introduces the basics of networking and NetWare via simple, generic overviews. The material given here is intended mainly for new NetWare users who need an overall, high-level orientation.

I suggest that you include this chapter in all your user materials, because it provides the background context for further training. However, feel free to customize the information based on how your network is set up and administered, what you want to teach your users, and what they already know. Ideas for doing this are included throughout the text.

What is a Network?

Explains what networks are and why they're useful.

A network is a group of computers connected together so that the people using them can communicate and share resources. Networks can greatly increase an organization's efficiency and cost-effectiveness.

Template: An Overview of Our Network

You can use the following template to give users a very general overview of how you're using networks. Modify the template to suit your needs.

At <substitute your organization name here>, we use networks to <list purposes of your network—link personal computers, access on-line services, etc.>.

Our network spans <physical area the network covers—building, nationwide, international, etc.> There are <number> of <type> computers connected to our network.

About <number> people from <number or names of> divisions work on the network. On our networks, we're doing <describe the kind of work being done on your networks>.

We decided to use networks because <list your reasons for implementing networks>. We've been using networks since <general time period when you first installed networks at your organization>. We plan to <describe future plans for networking in your organization—keep it pretty general at this point>.

Essential Network Components

Explains the essential components of a NetWare network and what they do.

Networks vary greatly in their actual physical setup and complexity. But regardless of their size or complexity, all NetWare networks have at least the following essential components:

File servers—personal computers which store network applications and network data. (Application—software which manages specialized tasks, like word processing or accounting.)

You may wish to list some applications which your users are familiar with as examples here.

File servers also run the NetWare operating system, which manages the network's operation. (Operating system—software which manages a computer's inner workings so you can use the computer's services.)

Ideas for presenting and customizing this material:

(A template which you can use to customize users' written manuals is found on page 27.)

- Show users a file server.
- Tell users how many file servers are on your network.
- Tell users what applications are being used on your network.
- Include or delete the definition of "application" and "operating system" depending on your users' level of experience and what you want to teach them.

Workstations—personal computers where you and other network users do your work. Workstations enable you to access the applications and data which are on the file server. Workstations then run the applications and process the data using their own operating systems.

Workstations also run a piece of software called the NetWare shell, which decides if requests made at the workstation should be handled by the workstation's operating system or by NetWare, and routes the requests accordingly.

Ideas for presenting and customizing this material:

(A template which you can use to customize the users' written manuals is on page 27.)

- Show users some of the workstations on your network, or explain where they are (on individual desks, grouped according to functions, etc.) Tell them where the workstation(s) they'll be using are located.

- Tell users how many workstations are on the network.

- Tell users what network applications they'll be using and how they will access those applications (or tell them that you'll be covering this information and when you'll be covering it).

- Tell users what operating system the workstation runs (DOS in most cases), and that they can still use most of the commands they would use if they were using that machine as a standalone personal computer.

Network adapters—printed circuit boards which are inserted into every file server and workstation on the network.

LAN drivers—software which, along with network adapters, prepares information to travel between file servers and workstations.

Cabling and other hardware—physically connects the workstations and file servers into a network.

Ideas for presenting and customizing this material:

(A template which you can use to customize the users' written manuals is found on page 27.)

• Show a network adapter; explain how it's inserted into a PC.

• Show how network adapters are connected to cabling to attach a station to the network.

• Show users the hardware your network uses (cabling, BNC connectors, passive/active hubs, MAUs, etc.).

Network Peripherals

Explains peripherals and introduces common network peripherals.

Peripherals are physical resources that are part of the network. Peripherals are optional; the network can run without them. But some peripherals are essential for most network users—printers are a good example. Peripherals may be located throughout the network.

Common peripherals include:

• **Printers**

• **Disk subsystems**—external hard disks attached to the file server to expand its disk space.

• **Uninterruptible power supplies**—provide temporary power to the file server if the regular power supply goes off unexpectedly, and protect the server against power fluctuations.

• **Tape backup units**—back up network files.

Ideas for presenting and customizing this material:

(A template which you can use to customize the users' written manuals is on page 27.)

• Tell users what peripherals your network has, what services the peripherals provide, and which peripherals they'll use.

• Tell them where the printers are (especially the printers they'll be using).

Template: A Description of Our Network

You can use the following template to give users a description of your network. Modify the template to suit your needs.

A Description of Our Network

Here's a quick description of our network.

File Servers: <number and hardware type>

Connection hardware:

Network adapters: <type—Ethernet, Arcnet, etc.>

Cabling scheme: <type—Token ring, Star, etc.>

Peripherals: <list peripherals and purpose of each; tell users which they will use; if necessary, also list location, especially for peripherals like printers>

Workstations: <number and type on network>

Workstation you will use: <type, location>

Workstation operating system:

Applications on the network: <general (word processing, spreadsheets, etc.) or specific (WordPerfect, 1-2-3, etc.)>

Applications you will use: <specific applications the user will use>

Conclusion

Summarize what you covered and introduce what will be covered next. A sample conclusion for this generic chapter is included next. Change it based on how you changed the chapter.

Now you know what a network is and what our network is like. The next step is to learn how to work on the network, starting with logging in.

Logging In and Out

The text for this boilerplate chapter is found in
LOGIN.WP (WordPerfect version)
LOGIN.ASC (ASCII version)

CHAPTER 2

Getting On and Off the Network: Logging In and Out

> This chapter explains how to log in and out and how to change a password. (Account and other restrictions are explained in the next chapter.)

Why You Have to Log In

Before you can use the network, you must log in. Requiring you to log in is the network's way of identifying you so it can enforce network security and track your network activity. Logging in is the first level of NetWare security, since it controls who may access the network. Once you've logged in, you can work on the network within the limits of your network security and other restrictions.

> The instructions in this chapter assume that your users
>
> • Know where the CTRL, ALT, and DEL keys are located on their keyboards
>
> • Know what it means to boot a computer
>
> • Are at least somewhat familiar with working on a computer (they know they must press ENTER to execute a command, etc.)
>
> If you have novice users who are brand new to personal computers, you may need to add some material to this chapter.

How to Log In

Here are the steps involved in logging in.

> Start with one of the basic approaches given next, then customize based on how your network is set up and how much information you want to give your users.

> Approach #1:
>
> I recommend this approach for new users who just want to get on the network and don't need to know much about what's going on. This explanation is tailored for use with the following AUTOEXEC.BAT file.
>
> Echo off
> IPX > NUL
> NET3 > NUL
> F:
> prompt pg
> Login username

1. Turn on your machine if necessary.

2. Press CTRL-ALT-DEL to boot your machine.

    When you do this, the machine loads the workstation's operating system and runs the AUTOEXEC.BAT file (if one exists), just as it would if it weren't on the network.

    After that, some commands will be executed automatically to establish a connection with the network and log you in. You will see some network information, and then you'll be prompted for your password.

3. Enter your password when prompted.

   If you enter your password incorrectly, the network won't log you in. If this happens, you will have to type

   > LOGIN *username*

   and then enter your password when prompted.

Approach #2:

I recommend this approach for curious users who need to learn how to log in, but also want to know what's going on. This explanation is tailored for use with the following AUTOEXEC.BAT file.

Echo off
IPX
NET3
f:
Prompt pg
Login username

---

1. Turn on your machine.

2. Press CTRL-ALT-DEL to boot your machine.

   When you do this, the machine loads the workstation's operating system and runs the AUTOEXEC.BAT file (if one exists).

   What you'll see next is explained in the following table.

What You See	What It Means
A>IPX	IPX, the software that allows the network adapter to talk to the shell, is being loaded.
Version, revision, and copyright information for IPX	
A>NETX	NET2, NET3, or NET4 is loaded next, depending on the version of DOS that you're using. This is the portion of the shell that communicates with DOS.
Version, revision, and copyright information for NETX	
Attached to server *Servername* Date Time	The server you've attached to and when you attached to it.
A>F:	A pointer is being set up to the area of the file server's hard disk where the commands that let you log in are located.
F:\LOGIN>login *username* Enter your password:	You are being logged in as user *username* and now need to enter your password.

3. Enter your password to finish logging in.

   If you enter your password incorrectly, the network won't log you in. If this happens, you will have to type

   LOGIN *username*

   and then enter your password as prompted.

Approach #3: Logging In Manually

I don't recommend this approach. It doesn't make much sense to have users log in manually when you can use an AUTOEXEC.BAT file. But if you choose not to create an AUTOEXEC.BAT file for some reason, use this explanation.

1. Turn on your machine.

2. Press CTRL-ALT-DEL to boot your machine.

   When you do this, the machine does everything it would do even if you weren't using it on the network. It performs a self-check, runs the CONFIG.SYS file, and loads COMMAND.COM.

3. Type

       IPX

   This loads IPX, the software that allows the network adapter to talk to the shell.

4. Type

       ANET2
       ANET3
       ANET4

Choose the appropriate command for the version of DOS the user is using: ANET2 for DOS 2.X, ANET3 for DOS 3.X, ANET4 for DOS 4.X. Then delete the other two commands.

This step loads the NetWare shell, that communicates between DOS and NetWare.

5. Type

>F:

This points you to the area of the file server's hard disk that contains the commands you need to log in.

6. Type

>LOGIN *username*

7. Enter your password.

What You See After You Log In

You can take several approaches here.

1. Simply tell users what they'll see when they log in.

2. Explain why they see what they see when they log in.

3. Do something in between.

   In addition, it's very likely that you will need to customize this section according to what you have done with batch files, login scripts, and menus. This section consists of building blocks along with ideas for when each building block might be used. Pick, choose, and modify according to your needs.

Batch Files and Login Scripts

> This section explains how batch files and login scripts determine what users see when they log in. Include it if you have curious users who are sophisticated enough to understand the information and would like to learn about it—especially users who might like to tinker with their own login scripts and batch files. (Provided, of course, that you are comfortable with them doing so.)

Several files determine what you see after you log in.

- **Login scripts** contain commands that help prepare your workstation to work with NetWare. There are several types of login scripts: a system login script, which applies to everyone, and your personal login script, which applies to you alone.

> Technically speaking, there is also a third type of login script. A default login script is actually part of the LOGIN.EXE program. The default login script is executed if a user doesn't have a personal login script. It is the same login script you see when you log in as Supervisor for the first time. Users probably don't need to know about this login script.

When you log in, the system login script is executed first. Then your personal login script is executed.

- **Batch files** provide a convenient way of executing commands in "bunches." When the batch file's name is typed, the commands it contains are executed. Batch files provide a convenient shortcut; if a certain series of commands is executed routinely, it can be put in a batch file to automate the process.

> If you want, you can show users their login scripts and batch files now. However, you might want to save this until after they have taken a look around the network.

A Basic Display

This section explains the basic display that is set up by the default login script as part of the LOGIN.EXE program. This default login script is executed if a user doesn't have a personal login script. If there is a system login script, but no personal login script, this default login script will fill in any "holes" that the system login script leaves out.

It's unlikely that a user would see a display exactly like that explained in this section, but you can use the information given here as a starting point to explain what the user does see. You can also customize this section.

To customize this section so it shows the display the user really sees,

1. Log in as the user.

2. Create a screen dump in the file DISPLAY by typing

   CAPTURE CR=DISPLAY

   (Note: the user must have the Create right in the
    current directory for this to work)

3. Press the SHIFT and PRT SC keys simultaneously.

4. Retrieve the file DISPLAY into this section (SHIFT F10, filename for WordPerfect users).

5. Clean up the display by deleting the extraneous parts of the screen dump. HINT: Setting margins to .1, .1 eliminates unwanted doublespacing.

If you customize this section to show the actual screen display that the user sees, you may also want to customize the following generic explanation. (Note that this explanation assumes that users know what directory structures are; if they don't, you may want to skip over it and tell them that you'll explain the display later.)

Here's what you see when you log in, and what it means.

Display	**Meaning**
Good evening, *USERNAME*.	A greeting to you.
Drive A: maps to a local disk.	These are drive mappings. Drive mappings point to different storage areas on the file server's hard disk.
Drive B: maps to a local disk.	
Drive C: maps to a local disk.	
Drive D: maps to a local disk.	
Drive E: maps to a local disk.	
Drive F: = LATE\SYS: \	
SEARCH1: = Z:. [LATE\SYS: \PUBLIC]	These are search drive mappings. They tell the system where to look if it can't find a file you request in your current directory.
SEARCH2: = Y:. [LATE\SYS: \]	

Custom Menus

If you have created a custom menu that is displayed when the user logs in, explain the menu here.

The next few sections contain examples of some simple custom menus you might use. They also explain how to create these menus with the NetWare MENU utility, then call the menus from the user's login script.

Here's a quick refresher on how to create a menu with NetWare's MENU utility, then call the menu from a login script so it will appear when the user logs in.

1. Make a text file to create the menu. Observe these rules:

   Menu title—first in the file, preceded by a % sign, flush left

   Menu options—Type flush left

   What the option does—type immediately following option, indented

2. Save the file in ASCII format with a .MNU extension.

3. Include this command at the end of the user's login script:

   #MENU *filename*

Notes on menus for supervisors:

If users can't access the files that create their menus, program execution will fail when the menu is called. For a user to access a file,

1. The .MNU file that creates the menu must be in the user's current directory or a directory mapped to a search drive.

2. The user must have Read and File Scan rights for the .MNU file.

If you will be using lots of menus, you may want to create a specific directory for .MNU files. Then, in the system login script, map a search drive to that directory, and use SYSCON to give the group EVERYONE Read and File Scan rights in the directory.

Sample Menu #1: Applications

This section explains how to create a simple menu that users can use to access their applications. This is a good menu for users that you want to shield from NetWare as much as possible.

The explanation of how to create the menu is given on this page. This explanation is for you, as supervisor, and should not be included in the user's manual. The explanation to include in the user's manual follows this explanation.

To create a custom menu to access applications, complete these steps.

1. First, make an ASCII text file to create the menu. Here is the basic format to use:

```
%MenuTitle
    Application1
    Echo off
    CLS
    command to access application1
Application2
    Echo off
    CLS
    command to access application2
Logout
    !logout
```

For example:

```
%Applications I Use
WordPerfect
    Echo off
    CLS
    WP
Lotus 1-2-3
    Echo off
    CLS
    123
Logout
    !logout
```

2. Save this file as an ASCII file with a .MNU extension—for example, APPS.MNU.

3. Call the menu from the user's login script by using this command at the end of the login script:

   #MENU *path:filename*

   For example, to call the menu created by APPS.MNU, at the end of the user's login script, include this command:

   #MENU *path:APPS*

> Explanation to include in user's manual for Sample Menu #1:
>
> This is the explanation you would include in the user manual—customized to your particular menu, of course.

Use the following menu to access your applications:

<Type the menu here, just as it appears to the user>

<After the menu, explain each menu item—what it is, why and how it would be used, etc.>

When you are finished working in your application, exit as usual. You are returned to this menu.

When you are finished working, highlight the "Logout" option and press ENTER to exit the system.

Sample Menu #2: Applications ... and then some

In the previous example, all of the user's files are dumped into the same directory—wherever the user was when the applications were accessed.

This example shows how to create a menu that automatically moves the user to a given directory when an application is accessed. That way, you can ensure that all files of a certain type are placed in the same directory.

This example is probably a little simple-minded in actual practice, but it illustrates the basic principle. Modify it to suit your needs.

Here is the explanation for you, as supervisor. Do not include this explanation in the user's manual—unless you want the user to be able to create his or her own menus.

To create a custom menu used to access applications, and that moves the user to a given directory upon accessing a certain application, complete these steps.

1. First, make an ASCII text file to create the menu. Here's the basic format to use:

%MenuTitle
Application1
   Echo Off
   CLS
   CD *desired directory*
   command to access application1
Application2
   Echo Off
   CLS

        CD *desired directory*
        command to access application2
   Logout
      !logout

For example:

%Diana's Menu
     WordPerfect
     Echo Off
     CLS
     CD \Home\Diana\WPfiles
     WP
  Lotus 1-2-3
     Echo Off
     CLS
     CD \Home\Diana\123files
     123
  Logout
     !logout

2. Save this file as an ASCII file with a .MNU extension—for example, DIANA.MNU.

3. Call the menu from the user's login script by using this command at the end of the login script:

#MENU *path:filename*

For example, to call the menu created by DIANA.MNU, at the end of the user's login script, include this command:

#MENU SYS:MENUS:DIANA

Explanation to include in user's manual for Sample Menu #2:

This is the explanation you would include in the user manual—customized to your particular menu, of course. It is the same as the explanation for the previous menu, because to the user, the two menus look about the same.

Use the following menu to access your applications:

<Type the menu here, just as it appears to the user>

<After the menu, explain each menu item—what it is, why and how it would be used, etc.>

When you are finished working in your application, exit as usual. You are returned to this menu.

When you are finished working, highlight the "Logout" option and press ENTER to exit the system.

Sample Menu #3: The NetWare Menu Utilities

This example explains how to create a simple menu which users can use to access the most commonly-used NetWare menu utilities. If you want to limit your users' access to the NetWare interface, and feel that menu utilities are the best bet, you might use a menu similar to the one in this section. (In actual practice, you would probably also include options to access applications— making your real menu a combination of this menu and a menu in one of the previous examples.)

You can choose which utilities you want to include in the menu, of course. I've included SYSCON, SESSION, FILER, and PCONSOLE in the example, but SYSCON and FILER are sufficient for most users.

Here is the explanation for you, as supervisor. Do not include this explanation in the user's manual—unless you want the user to be able to create his or her own menus.

To create a custom menu used to access the NetWare menu utilities, complete the steps on the next page.

1. First, make an ASCII text file to create the menu.

   ```
   %NetWare Utilities
   SYSCON
           Echo off
           CLS
           SYSCON
   FILER
           Echo off
           CLS
           FILER
    SESSION
           Echo off
           CLS
           SESSION
    PCONSOLE
           Echo off
           CLS
           PCONSOLE
    Logout
           !logout
   ```

2. Save this file with a .MNU extension—for example, NETUTILS.MNU.

3. Call the menu from the user's login script by using this command at the end of the login script:

   #MENU *path:NETUTILS*

Explanation to include in user's manual for Sample Menu 3:

Here are some ideas of what you might want to include in the user's manual if you had created a menu just like the one in the previous example.

Use this menu to access the NetWare menu utilities.

To access a utility, use the arrow keys to highlight it. Then press ENTER.

When you are finished working in the utility, exit by pressing ESCAPE and answering "Yes" when prompted to exit the utility. You are then returned to this menu.

When you are finished working, highlight the "Logout" option and press ENTER to exit the system.

Here you may include documentation for the utilities themselves if you wish. You can copy what you want from the reference chapter on the NetWare menu utilities, and place it here. If you do this, you may want to eliminate the menu utilities and command line utilities reference sections from the user's manual.

Logging In to More than One Server at a Time

Include this section only if

- There is more than one file server on the network.

- The user has an account on more than one of the servers

Sometimes you may need to work on more than one server at a time. If this is the case, you'll need to log in to all the servers you need to work on. Here is how to do so.

1. Log in to your regular server as usual.

2. If you know the name of the server you want to log in to, and your username on that server, type

    ATTACH *servername/username*

    For example, if you wanted to attach to server GADFLY as user Steve, type

    ATTACH GADFLY/STEVE

    If you don't know the name of the server, use the SLIST command to list the servers on the network. Type

    SLIST

    You'll see a list of servers on the network. Pick the server you want to log in to, then type

    ATTACH *servername/username*

3. You'll probably be prompted for a password after you enter your username. Enter the password at the prompt.

How to Change Your Password

There are several ways to change your password.

> Include the ways that are relevant.
>
> 1. Include either the menu or command line method depending whether your users use menu or command line NetWare commands.
>
> 2. If you don't force password changes, delete the next paragraph.

- **Forced change.** On our network, you must change your password periodically. The network tells you when you need to change your password. You'll get a message telling you that your password has expired. When you are prompted to enter a new password, type your new password at the "Enter new password" prompt; then re-type it when prompted. You must observe any password restrictions that apply, such as minimum length or uniqueness.

> You may or may not want to tell your users about grace logins, if they apply. The disadvantage in doing so is that if users know about grace logins, they tend to put off changing their passwords and then get locked out.
>
> If you want to tell users about grace logins, you can use the following sample text.

When you are prompted to change your password, you have a certain number of "grace" logins during which you can still use the old password to log in. Once you run out of grace logins, you will be locked out from the server. For this reason, it is best to make a habit of changing your password right away.

- **Voluntary change.** Sometimes you will want to change your password of your own accord.

Include this method if users have access to the command line.

To change your password voluntarily,

1. Type

    SETPASS

2. Enter your new password when prompted.

3. Re-enter your new password when prompted.

Include this method if users only have access to the menu utilities.

1. Access SYSCON.

2. Choose "User Information."

3. Choose your name.

4. Choose "Change Password."

5. Enter your new password.

6. Re-enter your new password.

Logging Out

When you are finished working on the network, you should always log out—just like you lock the door when you leave the house so intruders cannot get in. In fact, you should log out from the network if you're going to leave your workstation for any length of time. This prevents potentially malicious users from using network resources or accessing your personal data.

> Include this method if users log out from the command line.

To log out, type

      LOGOUT

You see a message telling you when you logged out and what server(s) you logged out from.

> Include this method if users log out from a custom menu and you haven't already covered how to log out when you explained how to use the menu.

To log out,

1. Use the arrow keys to highlight the "Logout" option.

2. Press ENTER.

   You see a message telling you when you logged out and what server(s) you logged out from.

Conclusion

> The following sample conclusion and transition is based on the generic information in this chapter. If you include it, modify it according to how you modified the chapter and what you will cover next.

In this chapter, you learned

- How to log in to the network

- What you see when you log in to the network

- How to use batch files and login scripts

- How to use menus

- How to attach to another file server

- How to change your password

- How to log out

Now that you have logged in, we'll start looking around the network.

CHAPTER OVERVIEW

Network Restrictions

The text for this boilerplate chapter is found in
RESTRICT.WP (WordPerfect version)
RESTRICT.ASC (ASCII version)

CHAPTER 3

Network Restrictions

This chapter explains some of the restrictions that may apply to your users. (It does NOT explain security; security is explained in the next chapters.) The chapter is divided into two sections:

1. Account restrictions, which limit when and how users can log in.

2. Disk and volume restrictions, which limit how much space users can consume on the file server.

Choose the material you want to include based on the restrictions you have established for your network, and what you want your users to know about those restrictions.

Because a network is a shared environment, there are many restrictions that control how you work on it. This chapter explains the restrictions that apply to you on our network.

Section 1: Account Restrictions

Login Restrictions

If you have set up account restrictions, it is important to explain them to your users. This will save them the frustration of trying to log in during unauthorized time periods, etc. It may also save you the frustration of having to solve problems caused because users don't understand their restrictions.

On our network, there are some restrictions that affect when and how you can log in. You need to know about these restrictions so they won't get in your way.

You can take a couple of approaches to explaining the restrictions:

You can just tell your users what they are, or

You can show your users how to see the restrictions, then explain what they mean.

Sample sections for each approach are included next.

Approach #1 (Login Restrictions): Tell users what their login restrictions are.

This section lists login restrictions that might apply to users. Delete the restrictions that don't apply. Then insert the appropriate information as instructed by the notes within the angle brackets.

Here are the login restrictions that apply to you and what they mean.

While you are filling in the blanks in the next section, you may want to look at the information in SYSCON. To do so,

1. Access SYSCON.

2. Account restrictions—default or individual user

a. If you have established default account restrictions that apply to everyone on your server, choose "Supervisor Options." Then choose "Default Account Balance/ Restrictions."

b. If you have established account restrictions on a user-by-user basis, choose "User Information." Then choose the user name, and "Account Restrictions."

(If you have done this, you must modify the next section in each user's manual separately so that the manuals are accurate.)

Expiration date. After <insert the date here>, you won't be able to log in to the network any more.

Number of workstations. You can only be logged in to the file server from <insert the number of stations here> workstations at a time.

Password required. Passwords <are, aren't> required on our network.

Changing your password. You <can, cannot> change your own password.

Minimum Password Length. Your password must be at least <number> characters long.

Periodic password changes. You must change your password every <number> days. You will be prompted when it's time to change your password.

Grace logins. When it comes time to change your password, it's best to do so right away. You will still be allowed <number> grace logins, when you can still log in with the old password. If you don't change your password before your grace logins are used up, you will be unable to log in to the network. Then you'll have to come to <name of their supervisor, account manager, workgroup manager, help desk, etc.> for help.

Unique passwords. You <can, cannot> use a password you've used before.

Station restrictions. You can only log in from certain workstations. <Tell them which ones.>

Time restrictions. You can only log in to the network and use it during the following time periods:

<List the time periods here. Modify the following sample text.>

<u>Day</u>	<u>Time</u>
Sun	
Mon	
Tues	
Weds	
Thurs	
Fri	
Sat	

Approach #2: (Login Restrictions) Tell users how to see their login restrictions and explain what the restrictions mean as they go along.

NOTE: This approach will work only if you have set up account restrictions for the user specifically, using the "User Information" option in SYSCON. If you have used the "Supervisor Options" option to set up restrictions for all users, users will not be able to see the restrictions because they cannot access the information under the "Supervisor Options" menu option.

To see your login restrictions, choose the method that applies or modify as desired.

• At the DOS prompt, type SYSCON and press ENTER.
or
• Choose SYSCON from the menu.

1. Choose "User Information."

2. Choose your name.

3. Choose "Account Restrictions."

Here are the restrictions that apply to you and what they mean.

Disable account. Your account can be disabled so that you cannot log in, but this is rare.

Expiration date. If this says "Yes," you won't be able to log in after the date specified under "Date Account Expires."

Limit Concurrent Connections. If this says "Yes," you can only be logged in to the number of workstations specified under "Maximum Connections."

Allow User to Change Password. If this says "Yes," you can change your password.

Require Password. If this says "Yes," you must enter a password to log in. The restrictions that apply to your password are next:

> **Minimum Password Length.** The number of characters your password must be.

> **Force Periodic Password Changes.** If you select "Yes," you must change your password periodically. The amount of time between password changes is shown in the next field, "Days Between Forced Changes." The date your password expires, and if you will have to specify a new one, is shown in the field "Date Password Expires."

> **Limit Grace Logins.** If this says "Yes," you have a certain number of "grace" logins when you can still use the old password before changing it. The number of grace logins is shown next to "Grace Logins Allowed," and the number you have left is shown next to "Remaining Grace Logins."

> **Require Unique Passwords.** If this says "Yes," you cannot use a password you've used before when you specify a new password.

5. Now press ESCAPE.

6. Choose "Station Restrictions."

This shows you the addresses of the workstations you're allowed to log in from.

> Unfortunately, station addresses don't mean much to most users. If you have restricted the workstations they can log in from, it is probably best to just tell them where they are allowed to log in from.

7. Press ESCAPE.

8. Choose "Time Restrictions."

This shows you the times you are allowed to log in. The time periods that have asterisks are the time periods when you can log in or be logged in; the time periods without asterisks are the time periods when you cannot log in or be logged in on the network.

9. Press ALT-F10 and answer "Yes" to exit SYSCON.

Section 2: Disk and Volume Restrictions

Disk and Volume Restrictions

Include this section if

- You have limited the disk and/or volume space available to the user.

- You wish to tell the user about this restriction.

This section offers the same approaches as before:

1. Tell the user what the restrictions are.

2. Tell the user how to see the restrictions and what they mean.

3. A third alternative that allows users to automatically monitor their restrictions is also explained.

Approach #1: (Disk and Volume Restrictions)

Tell users what their restrictions are.

On our network, there are some restrictions on how much total disk space you can use.

Here are the restrictions that apply to you:

On file server <server name>, you can use <number> Kilobytes of space.

On volume <insert the volume name here>, you can use <insert number here> Kilobytes of space.

The directory <insert directory name here> can only use <insert number here> Kilobytes of space.

If you reach any of these limits, you won't be able to save files. You will have to go back and delete some of your old files to free up space before you can save files again.

Approach #2: (Disk and Volume Restrictions)

Show users how to see their restrictions and explain what they mean as you go along.

On our network, there are some restrictions on how much total disk space you can use.

To see your space restrictions:

1. At the DOS prompt, type

   DSPACE

2. Choose "User Restrictions."

3. Choose your name.

4. Choose <insert the appropriate volume name here>.

5. You'll then see how much space is available to you.

If you use up all of your space, you won't be able to save files. You will have to go back and delete your old files to free up some space before you can save files again.

Include the next section if you have placed space limitations on certain directories and want users to be aware of those restrictions.

Some of the directories on our file server also have space limitations placed on them. To see those limitations,

6. Press Escape three times to return to the "Available Options" menu.

7. Choose "Directory Restrictions."

8. Specify the directory.

   Press Insert and choose directories until you're where you want to be.

9. Press Escape.

10. Press Enter.

11. The space limit placed on the directory, and the amount of space currently available in the directory, will then be shown.

If this space limit is reached, you won't be able to save files in this directory. You will have to go back and delete some files to free up space before you can save files again.

Approach #3: (Disk and Volume Restrictions)

Forcing users to check periodically

The main reason to tell users about their restrictions is so they won't run out of space—or so that if they do, they'll know what's going on. Of course, it's better to be proactive than reactive. There are a couple of ways to do this.

You can use SYSCON to monitor network usage yourself. Then, when users approach their space limits, send a warning to tell them they're running out of space and need to delete their old files.

You can also include CHKVOL in users' login scripts to force them to check their restrictions themselves. This sections explains how to do so and gives you a template to use in your manuals if you take this approach.

Of course, if you give users this responsibility, you should make sure they're up to it. It won't help them much to know that they're approaching their space limit if they don't have the Erase right in at least some of the directories they work in, because they won't be able to clean up old files anyway. And no matter what your users' level of expertise, if you force them to check their restrictions, you should educate them properly so they know when they must check their restrictions, how they should do so, and what to do when they're approaching the limit.

How to Force Users to Check their Space Usage Periodically

The following sequence of commands can be used in the system login script to force all users to check space restrictions at least monthly:

IF DAY=*"day"* THEN BEGIN

    WRITE "It's time to check your disk restrictions. You will be shown"
    WRITE "some statistics about your file server's disk volumes. The"
    WRITE "fourth line shows how much disk space you have left."
    PAUSE
    CHKVOL *
    PAUSE

END

(Substitute the desired number—01, 12, 28, etc.—for *"day"* in the IF...THEN command that begins the above sequence.)

Always include this command sequence at the END of a login script, because once the external program execution command (#CHKVOL) is executed, the rest of the login script will be skipped over.

The command sequence given above can be modified to suit your needs. You can include any message in the WRITE commands; you can also have users check weekly, if you want. To do so, just substitute this line for the first line given above:

IF DAY_OF_WEEK= *"day"* THEN BEGIN

(Substitute the desired day—Monday, Wednesday, Thursday, etc.—for *day* in the above command)

Template for Approach #3 (Disk and Volume Restrictions)

Here is the template to include in your user manuals. If you use it, you may want to move it from this chapter to the section in Chapter 2 entitled "What You See When You Log In."

On our network, the amount of disk space you can use has been restricted. If you reach your space limits, you will have to delete some of your old files before you can save files or run some programs again.

So that you don't run into problems, you will be forced to check your space restrictions periodically. When you log in on <list the day of the month or day of the week you used in the IF...THEN statement in the user's login script>, you'll see this message:

<Include the message from the WRITE command in the login script here>

Then the CHKVOL utility, that is used to check your restrictions, is automatically executed.

If you are approaching your limit, take a minute to clean up your directories. List your files, and delete those that you no longer need. You may find the following commands useful as you do this.

Command	Purpose
NDIR REV SORT UPDATE	Sorts files from most- to least-recently updated, making it easy to see which files are old
NDIR REV SORT ACCESS	Sorts files from most- to least-recently accessed, making it easy to see which files you've looked at recently
NDIR SORT SIZE	Sorts files from smallest to largest, making it easy to see what is taking up the most space

Conclusion

> The following sample conclusion and transition is based on the generic information in this chapter. If you include it, modify it according to how you modified the chapter and what you plan to cover next.

In this chapter, you learned about your network login and disk restrictions. These included

1) Restrictions that control when, where, and how you log in

2) Restrictions on how much disk and volume space you can use on the file server

In the next chapter, you will learn how to work with directories and files. You will also learn about network security restrictions.

Working With Directories and Files

Chapters 4 and 5 explain how to work with directories and files. They cover basically the same ground. However, Chapter 4 explains how to complete tasks with the NetWare Command Line utilities, while Chapter 5 explains how to complete tasks with the NetWare Menu utilities.

Generally, the Command Line utilities are best for experienced users who perform a particular task often, and prefer speed and flexibility; the Menu utilities are best for novice users or those who perform a particular task infrequently, and need to be guided along.

You may want to skim quickly through the chapters before deciding on your approach. You may also want to combine material from each chapter to create your own custom chapter.

4

Working With Directories and Files (Command Line Utilities Version)

The text for this boilerplate chapter is found in
FILESCLU.WP (WordPerfect version)
FILESCLU.ASC (ASCII version)

Working with Directories and Files

Command Line Utilities Version

This chapter explains how to work with directories and files. It explains concepts, such as how directory structures and drive mappings work; and how to complete basic tasks, such as creating directories, copying files, and deleting files.

As with the rest of the Manual Maker, the approach you take in this chapter depends on how you have set up your network, how experienced your users are, and how much you want to teach them.

Directory Structures

This section explains directory structures and how they work.

A network contains a lot of information. Without some sort of organization, that information is very difficult to work with. But rest assured, there is an effective way to organize network information.

The information on a file server's hard disk is organized by the file server's directory structure, a type of electronic filing system. A directory structure is made up of directories, areas of the hard disk that contain files and other directories. Directories are placed inside other directories, forming a branching, tree-like structure. (In fact, directory structures are often called directory trees.) Files are then organized by placing them inside the directory structure.

Directories have special names that describe their relationship to each other in the structure:

A **volume**, the highest level in the structure, is an actual physical area on the hard disk. All directories are subdivisions of the volume.

The **root directory** is the volume level. The root directory is designated by a backslash (\). It contains all of the other directories on the volume.

A directory's **parent directory** is the directory immediately above the directory.

The current, or **default**, directory is your current location in the directory structure. NetWare and DOS both look for data and program files in this directory first. If another directory isn't specified, this directory is assumed.

A **subdirectory** of a directory is any directory located below that directory.

A Sample Directory Structure

Here is part of a sample directory structure. The levels in this structure are labeled in parentheses at the bottom of the diagram.

> If you want to substitute an actual directory structure from your server, go ahead. I used this one because it corresponds closely to how many users' home directories are set up.
>
> If you use an actual directory structure in this example, use the same directory structure in the next example too.

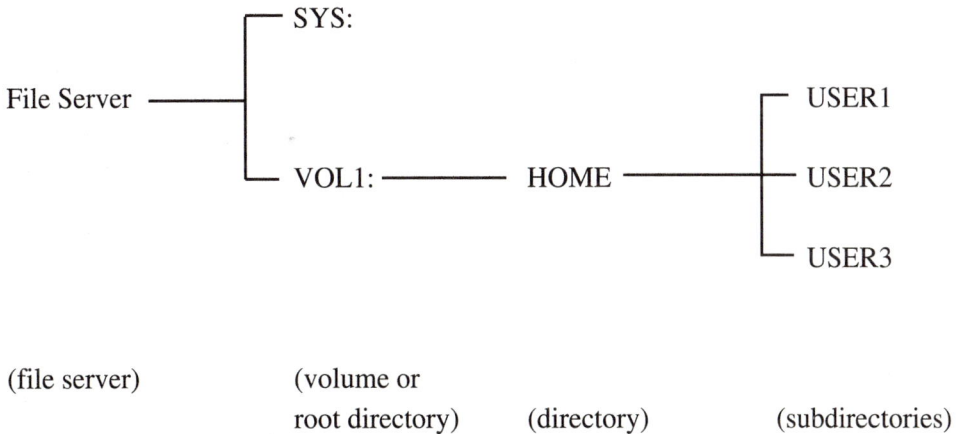

```
                         ┌─ SYS:

File Server  ───────┤                                    ┌─ USER1

                         └─ VOL1: ───────── HOME ──────────┼─ USER2

                                                          └─ USER3
```

(file server)   (volume or
                     root directory)   (directory)   (subdirectories)

Directory Paths

> This section explains directory paths and directory names.

To find a file, you must know where it is located in the directory structure. A file's location is indicated by its directory path, or "path" for short. The path consists of the file server, volume, root directory, and any other directories leading up to the file.

Here is the same directory structure you saw before, with a directory path indicated by asterisks.

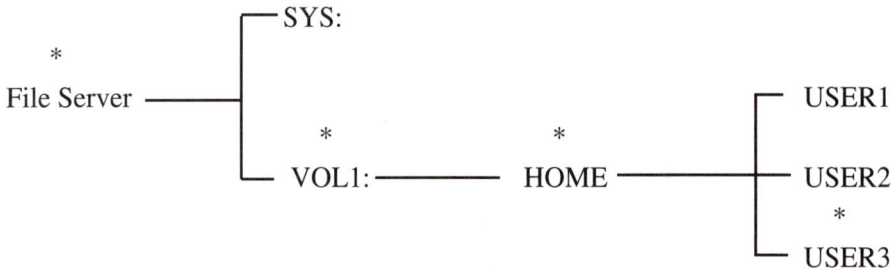

```
                      ┌─ SYS:
        *             │                                        ┌─ USER1
   File Server ───────┤                                        │
                      │        *              *                │
                      └─ VOL1:────────── HOME ─────────────────┤   USER2
                                                               │      *
                                                               └─ USER3
```

The path indicated by the asterisks would be specified as follows:

FILESERVER\VOL1:HOME\USER3

Getting an Overview of the Directory Tree

This section explains how to get an overview of the directory tree.

Because NetWare security controls what you can see, you may not be able to see all areas of the directory tree. If your view of the tree is different than someone else's, it's because your security privileges are different from theirs.

Here's how to get an overview of the part of the directory tree which you can work with.

1. Move to the root directory by typing

   CD \

2. Type

   LISTDIR /S

You'll then see an overview of the directory tree, similar to what follows.

```
The sub-directory structure of LATE/SYS:
Directory
─────────────────────
LOGIN
PUBLIC
MAIL
    B00001B
DIANA
    MYM
    WORDPROC
MENU
WP51
9 sub-directories found
```

You can customize this section to show the exact directory tree which a user sees. Here's how:

1. Log in as the user.

2. Go to the root directory and type

    LISTDIR /S >*path*\DIRTREE

This redirects the output from the LISTDIR /S command to the file DIRTREE, which is created in the directory you specified in the path. For this reason, the user must have the Create right in that directory, or the file DIRTREE cannot be created.

3. Delete the example given here, and delete "similar to this" in the sentence that introduces the example.

4. Retrieve the file DIRTREE into the text here (SHIFT + F10, \DIRTREE).

Now that you've gotten an overview of the directory tree, we'll talk about NetWare security and how it controls what you can do with directories and files.

Approaches to NetWare Security

Network security is a fairly complex topic, and there are many possible approaches to it. In this section, I've offered you three. I recommend that you skim through all the explanations before deciding which approach to take. Then pick the one that comes closest to what you want, and modify as desired.

Network Security, Approach #1: Basic

This approach allows you to skirt the issue of security almost entirely. You simply tell users where they can work and what they can do. It's a bottom-line approach that does not even deal with the actual details of security, but simply explains the end results from a user's perspective. I recommend this approach for novice users.

If you choose this approach,

- Set up your security very carefully so that users won't run into problems.

- Test your security by logging in as the user and making sure that you can do everything you want the user to be able to do.

- Realize that the burden of troubleshooting security-related problems (that account for many common network problems) rests squarely on you, as supervisor.

NetWork Security

Network security determines what directories and files you can access on our network, and what you can do with those directories and files.

Following is a list of the directories you can work with on our network and what you can do in each directory.

List the directories where the user has security privileges (rights), and indicate what the user can do in each directory, based on what his or her rights are. You can do this as follows:

1. Log in as the user.
2. Move to a directory where the user has the Create right.
3. Type CLS to clear the screen.
4. At the DOS prompt, type
   WHOAMI /R >MYRIGHTS
5. Now retrieve the file MYRIGHTS into this document and remove any extraneous information.
6. Delete the file MYRIGHTS from the directory where you created it.

If you customize the preceding example, you should also explain it. The following example walks you through the process of customizing the example for user Diana, and gives you ideas and sample explanations. (Because the example is lengthy, I haven't put it into comments. You should delete most of this explanation from your user manuals, of course. However, you may want to modify portions of it for use in your manuals.)

To modify this Security section for user Diana, I would complete these steps.

1. Log in as Diana.

2. Move to Diana's personal directory, SYS:HOME\DIANA.

3. Type CLS.

4. Type

   WHOAMI /R >MYRIGHTS

5. Move to the appropriate place in this document.

6. Retrieve the file MYRIGHTS into this document (SHIFT F10, \HOME\DIANA\MYRIGHTS for WordPerfect users).

At this point, MYRIGHTS looks something like the following:

^^ ^P ^— ^Q ^^ ^ ^PYou are user DIANA attached to server LATE, connection 1.
Server LATE is running NetWare 386 V3.10 Rev. A.
Login time: Monday October 15, 1990 10:40 am

```
[              ]          SYS:
  [ R        F ]                SYS:LOGIN
  [ R        F ]                SYS:PUBLIC
  [   C      ]                SYS:MAIL
  [ RWCEMF  ]                SYS:MAIL/4000001
    [ RWCEMFA]                    SYS:HOME/DIANA
  [ R        F ]                SYS:WP51
```

7. Remove the extraneous characters and fix the spacing so that MYRIGHTS looks like this:

```
[              ]          SYS:
[ R        F ]          SYS:LOGIN
[ R        F ]          SYS:PUBLIC
[   C      ]          SYS:MAIL
[ RWCEM F ]          SYS:MAIL/4000001
[SRWCEMFA]          SYS:HOME/DIANA
[ R        F ]          SYS:WP51
```

8. Add explanations.

   You may want to comment on how the tree is organized and why it is organized that way. For example,

   A. Give a general explanation of each directory's purpose. (You may wish to delete the directories that you do not want to tell the user about—for example, most users do not need to know about directories such as SYS:LOGIN, SYS:PUBLIC, and SYS:MAIL.)

   B. Mention which directories contain applications and utilities, and which contain data files.

   C. Point out the user's home directory, if you have created one.

   D. Explain which directories contain shared files, such as database files, and tell who else has access to such directories.

   You should also tell the user what he or can do in each directory (create files, look at files, organize a structure beneath, etc.). Use the rights sets as your guide as you do this.

With explanations, the MYRIGHTS file now looks like this:

[SRWCEMFA]   SYS:DIANA   This is your personal directory. You have all security privileges here. You can list, create, delete, and modify files; create, delete, and rename directories; and assign security.

[R   F]   SYS:WP51   This directory contains the WordPerfect application files. Your security privileges allow you to run these files, but nothing else.

9. Delete the rights sets and adjust the spacing. After this step, the sample file MYRIGHTS looks similar to this (notice that I have not included explanations for all of the directories where the user has rights):

SYS:DIANA   This is your personal directory. You have all security privileges here. You can list, create, delete, and modify files; create, delete, and rename directories; and assign security.

SYS:WP51   This directory contains the WordPerfect application files. Your security privileges allow you to run these files, but nothing else.

Network Security, Approach #2: Intermediate

This approach deals briefly with security, explaining everything that most non-administrative users need to know. It is a middle-of-the road approach that covers only effective rights and how they determine what a user can do with a directory or file. I recommend it for most intermediate users.

If you choose this approach, you should still set up and test your security carefully. If security problems do come up, you will probably still have to help users, since they can not change their own security. But even so, I think it is worth teaching users a little about security, because many common problems are security-related (for example, not being able to run an application or save a file).

NetWare Security

Network security determines what directories and files you can access on our network, and what you can do with those directories and files.

Your network security is based on the security privileges that you are allowed to exercise in any given directory or for any given file. These are called your "effective rights." There are eight rights, and they are shown between brackets, like this:

[SRWCEMFA]

Each letter stands for a right that allows certain privileges, as summarized in the following table. Notice that sometimes the meaning of a right varies depending on what level it applies to (directory or file).

Letter	Right	Lets you ...
S	Supervisory	Exercise all rights for directory or file
R	Read	Directory level: Open a directory's files and read them or copy them to other directories
		File level: Open a file and read it or copy it to another directory
W	Write	Directory level: Change contents of files in directory
		File level: Change contents of file
C	Create	Directory level: Create files and subdirectories
		File level: Salvage deleted files; create and write a file
E	Erase	Directory level: Delete empty directories
		File level: Delete the file
M	Modify	Directory level: Change directory attributes; rename subdirectories and files
		File level: Change the file's attributes; re-name the file
F	File Scan	Directory level: See files and subdirectories
		File level: See the file
A	Access Control	Assign security for directory or file

Viewing Your Effective Rights Throughout the Directory Tree

To know what your security privileges allow you to do, you need to see your effective rights throughout the directory tree. To do so, type

LISTDIR /S /E

You see a display similar to this:

```
The sub-directory structure of LATE/SYS:
Effective          Directory

[ R    F ]         LOGIN
[ R    F ]         PUBLIC
[   C    ]         MAIL
[ RWCEMF ]          B00001B
[SRWCEMFA]         DIANA
[SRWCEMFA]           MYM
[SRWCEMFA]            WORDPROC
[ R    F ]         MENU
[ R    F ]         WP51
9 sub-directories found
```

You can customize this section to show exactly what a user sees. Here is how:

1. Log in as the user.

2. Go to the root directory and type

    LISTDIR /SUB >\path\RIGHTS

    Use a path leading up to a directory where the user has the Create right.

4. Delete the example given here, and delete "similar to this" in the sentence that introduces the example.

5. Retrieve the file RIGHTS into the text here (SHIFT + F10, \DIRTREE).

6. Clean the text up by removing extraneous characters, fixing spacing, etc.

If you customize this example, you should also explain it. The following example walks you through the process of customizing the example for user Diana, and gives you ideas and sample explanations. (Because the example is lengthy, I have not put it into comments. You should delete most of this explanation from your user manuals, of course. However, you may want to modify portions of it for use in your manuals.)

Example: Customizing the Security Section

To modify this security section for user Diana, I would complete these steps.

1. Log in as Diana.

2. Move to Diana's personal directory, SYS:HOME\DIANA.

3. Type CLS.

4. Type

   WHOAMI /R >MYRIGHTS

5. Move to the appropriate place in this document.

6. Retrieve the file MYRIGHTS into this document (SHIFT F10,
   \HOME\DIANA\MYRIGHTS). At this point, MYRIGHTS looks something
   like this:

^^ ^P ^— ^Q ^^ ^PYou are user DIANA attached to server LATE,
connection 1. Server LATE is running NetWare 386 V3.10 Rev. A.
Login time: Monday October 15, 1990 10:40 am
```
    [             ]      SYS:
     [ R        F  ]            SYS:LOGIN
     [ R              F  ]   SYS:PUBLIC
     [    C          ]        SYS:MAIL
     [ RWCEMF  ]            SYS:MAIL/4000001
      [ RWCEMFA]              SYS:HOME/DIANA
      [ R        F  ]        SYS:WP51
```

7. Remove the extraneous characters and fix the spacing so that MYRIGHTS looks
   like this:

```
    [             ]    SYS:
    [ R        F  ]    SYS:LOGIN
    [ R        F  ]    SYS:PUBLIC
    [    C        ]    SYS:MAIL
    [ RWCEMF  ]    SYS:MAIL/4000001
    [SRWCEMFA]      SYS:HOME/DIANA
    [ R        F  ]    SYS:WP51
```

8. Add explanations.

   You may want to comment on how the tree is organized and why it is organized that way. For example,

   A. Give a general explanation of each directory's purpose. (You may wish to delete the directories that you do not want to tell the user about—for example most users do not need to know about directories such as SYS:LOGIN, SYS:PUBLIC, and SYS:MAIL.)

   B. Mention which directories contain applications and utilities, and which contain data files.

   C. Point out the user's home directory, if you have created one.

   D. Explain which directories contain shared files, such as database files, and state who has access to such directories.

   You should also tell the user what he or can do in each directory (create files, look at files, organize a structure beneath, etc.). Use the rights sets as your guide when you do this.

With explanations, MYRIGHTS looks something like this:

[   ]   Diana has no rights in the SYS directory.

[R   F]   Diana has Read and File Scan rights in three direc
                                tories, LOGIN, PUBLIC, and WP51. Read allows
                                Diana to open files and read their contents of files,
                                and File Scan allows her to list the files. This
                                combination of rights lets Diana run executable
                                (program) files, which these directories contain.
                                She does not have any other rights because she
                                should not be able to delete, rename, or otherwise
                                modify these files.

[RWCEMF]   Diana has all rights but Supervisory and Access
                                Control in a directory beneath the MAIL directory,
                                which is assigned to her.

[C   ]   Diana has the Create right in the MAIL directory.
                                This creates a "drop-box" directory, where Diana
                                can only create files. The files created in this direc-
                                tory have to do with the NetWare electronic mail
                                system.

[SRWCEMFA]   Diana has all rights in her home directory (DIANA),
                                and the directories beneath it (MYM and
                                WORDPROC). Thus, she has all privileges here.

Checking Your Effective Rights for Individual Directories or Files

You have just learned how to see your effective rights throughout the directory tree. Sometimes, however, you want to check your effective rights just for your current directory, or for a particular file.

To check your rights for your current directory, type

RIGHTS

To check your rights for a particular file, type

RIGHTS *filename*

Network Security, Approach #3: Advanced

This approach offers a complete explanation of security, including effective rights, trustee rights, inherited rights masks, and attributes. Security can get fairly involved at this level, so I do not recommend this approach for many users; for most users, it is sufficient—and simpler—just to see their effective rights. However, you might want to take this approach if you have advanced users and:

• You have given them the Supervisory or Access Control right in some directories, and expect them to assign security in those directories.

• You want to train them to be as independent as possible.

• You expect them to troubleshoot.

NetWare Security

Network security determines what directories and files you can access on our network, and what you can do with those directories and files.

Your network security is based on the security privileges you are allowed to exercise in any given directory or for any given file. These are called your "effective rights." There are eight rights, shown here between brackets:

[SRWCEMFA]

Each letter stands for a right that allows certain privileges, as summarized in the following table. Notice that sometimes the meaning of a right varies depending on what level it has been assigned at (directory or file).

Letter	Right	Lets you ...
S	Supervisory	Exercise all rights for directory or file
R	Read	Directory level: Open a directory's files and read them or copy them to other directories
		File level: Open a file and read it or copy it to another directory
W	Write	Directory level: Change contents of files in directory
		File level: Change contents of file
C	Create	Directory level: Create files and subdirectories
		File level: Salvage deleted files; create and write a file
E	Erase	Directory level: Delete empty directories
		File level: Delete the file
M	Modify	Directory level: Change directory attributes; rename subdirectories and files
		File level: Change the file's attributes; re-name the file
F	File Scan	Directory level: See files and subdirectories
		File level: See the file
A	Access Control	Assign security for directory or file

Viewing Your Effective Rights Throughout the Directory Tree

To know what your security privileges allow you to do, you need to see your effective rights throughout the directory tree. To do so, type

LISTDIR /S /E

You see a display similar to this:

```
The sub-directory structure of LATE/SYS:
Effective        Directory
_____

[ R     F ]      LOGIN
[ R     F ]      PUBLIC
[   C     ]      MAIL
[ RWCEMF ]         B00001B
[SRWCEMFA]       DIANA
[SRWCEMFA]          MYM
[SRWCEMFA]          WORDPROC
[ R     F ]      MENU
[ R     F ]      WP51
 9 sub-directories found
```

You can customize this section to show exactly what a user sees. Here is how:

1. Log in as the user.

2. Go to the root directory and type

   LISTDIR /SUB >*path*\RIGHTS

   Use a path leading up to a directory where the user has the Create right.

4. Delete the example given here, and delete "similar to this" in the sentence that introduces the example.

5. Retrieve the file RIGHTS into the text here (SHIFT + F10, \DIRTREE).

6. Clean the text up by removing extraneous characters, fixing spacing, etc.

If you customize this example, you should also explain it. The following example walks you through the process of customizing the example for user Diana, and gives you ideas and sample explanations. (Because the example is lengthy, I have not put it into comments. You should delete most of this explanation from your users' manuals, of course. However, you may want to modify portions of it for use in your manuals.)

Example: Customizing the Security Section

To modify this security section for user Diana, I would complete these steps.

1. Log in as Diana.

2. Move to Diana's personal directory, SYS:HOME\DIANA.

3. Type CLS.

4. Type

WHOAMI /R >MYRIGHTS

5. Move to the appropriate place in this document.

6. Retrieve the file MYRIGHTS into this document (SHIFT F10, \HOME\DIANA\MYRIGHTS).

   At this point, MYRIGHTS looks something like this:

^^ ^P ^— ^Q ^^ ^PYou are user DIANA attached to server LATE,
connection 1.
 Server LATE is running NetWare 386 V3.10 Rev. A.
Login time: Monday October 15, 1990 10:40 am
[   ]   SYS:
 [R   F]   SYS:LOGIN
 [R   F]   SYS:PUBLIC
 [C   ]   SYS:MAIL
 [RWCEMF   ]   SYS:MAIL/4000001
    [RWCEMFA]   SYS:HOME/DIANA
 [R   F]   SYS:WP51

7. Remove the extraneous characters and fix the spacing so that MYRIGHTS looks like this:

[   ]   SYS:
[R   F]   SYS:LOGIN
[R   F]   SYS:PUBLIC
[C   ]   SYS:MAIL
[RWCEMF]   SYS:MAIL/4000001

[SRWCEMFA]   SYS:HOME/DIANA
[R   F]   SYS:WP51

8. Add explanations.

You may want to comment on how the tree is organized and why it is organized that way. For example,

A. Give a general explanation of each directory's purpose. (You may wish to delete the directories that you do not want to tell the user about—for example most users do not need to know about directories such as SYS:LOGIN, SYS:PUBLIC, and SYS:MAIL.)

B. Mention which directories contain applications and utilities, and which contain data files.

C. Point out the user's home directory, if you have created one.

D. Explain which directories contain shared files, such as database files, and tell who else has access to such directories.

You should also tell the user what he or she can do in each directory (create files, look at files, organize a structure beneath, etc.). Use the rights sets as your guide as you do this.

With explanations, MYRIGHTS looks something like this:

[   ]   Diana has no rights in the SYS directory.

[R   F]   Diana has Read and File Scan rights in three direc-
                                    tories, LOGIN, PUBLIC, and WP51. Read lets
                                    Diana open files and read their contents, and

File Scan lets her list the files. This combination of rights lets Diana run executable (program) files, which these directories contain. She does not have any other rights because she should not be able to delete, rename, or otherwise work with these files.

[RWCEMF]

Diana has all rights but Supervisory and Access Control in a directory beneath the MAIL directory, which is assigned to her.

[C]

Diana has the Create right in the MAIL directory. This creates a "drop-box" directory, where Diana can only create files. The files created in this directory have to do with the NetWare electronic mail system.

[SRWCEMFA]

Diana has all rights in her home directory (DIANA), and the directories beneath it (MYM and WORDPROC). Thus, she has all privileges here.

Checking Your Effective Rights for Individual Directories or Files

You have just learned how to see your effective rights throughout the directory tree. Sometimes, however, you want to check your effective rights for just your current directory, or for a particular file.

To check your rights for your current directory, type

RIGHTS

To check your rights for a particular file, type

RIGHTS *filename*

How Your Effective Rights Were Determined

Your effective rights are determined by the rights granted to you as a user (your "trustee rights"), and the rights which a directory allows to be exercised (its "inherited rights mask").

Trustee Rights. When you are explicitly given privileges in a directory or file, you are called a "trustee" and your rights are called your "trustee rights." Trustee rights are the main method of authorizing you to work with directories and files.

Trustee rights can be assigned at any level in the directory tree—even at the file level, though this is rare. Usually, trustee assignments are granted at the highest level that is appropriate in a directory structure. When you are given trustee rights for a directory or file, your effective rights for the directory or file are the same as your trustee rights.

You may be given trustee rights directly, as a user. You may also be given trustee rights indirectly, through security equivalences. There are several types of security equivalences: you may be security-equivalent to another user, or you may be a member of a group, which makes you security-equivalent to the group. It is very common to gain the majority of your trustee rights via membership in groups.

Trustee rights "trickle down" through the subdirectory tree beneath the directory where they were granted, giving you the same rights in the subdirectory tree as in the directory. Rights gained by inheritance from a trustee assignment further up the directory tree are called "inherited rights." However, inherited rights may be limited by inherited rights masks, explained next.

Inherited Rights Masks. An inherited rights mask filters all users' inherited rights for a directory or file. Masks prevent users from accidentally inheriting more rights than they should have for a file or directory. Masks are a safeguard, and should rarely be set. The default is for an inherited rights mask to allow all rights.

Inherited rights masks do not filter trustee rights (those explicitly granted in a directory or file). They only filter inherited rights (those which "trickled down" from a trustee assignment granted at a higher level in the directory tree). There is, however, one exception: the Supervisory right is never filtered. If you want to see how your effective rights for a directory or file were determined, you need to know several things:

1. Do you have trustee rights or inherited rights for the directory or file?

2. Does the directory or file's inherited rights mask filter any rights?

Usually, it is sufficient to know this information at the directory level.

Let's start by looking at your trustee assignments.

To see the trustee assignments you have been given in a directory as a user,

1. Access SYSCON.

2. Choose "User Information."

3. Choose your name.

4. Choose "Trustee Directory Assignments."

You then see the directories where you have been given trustee rights, and what those trustee rights are. These are also your effective rights for the directories, regardless of whether the directories' inherited rights masks filter rights, because inherited rights masks do not filter trustee rights.

To see the trustee assignments you have been given indirectly, via your membership in groups, you first need to know which groups you belong to. You can find this out by typing

WHOAMI /G

Once you know which groups you belong to, you need to find out what their trustee assignments are. To do so, complete the following steps.

1. Access SYSCON.

2. Choose "Group Information."

3. Choose one of the groups you belong to.

4. Choose "Trustee Directory Assignments."

   You then see the directories where the group has been given trustee rights, and what those trustee rights are. These are also the group's effective rights for the directories, regardless of whether the directories' inherited rights masks filter rights, because inherited rights masks do not filter trustee rights. You have the same trustee rights as the group, since you are a member of it.

The trustee rights you have been given in a directory then trickle down through its subdirectory tree. These rights are your inherited rights for these subdirectories. Unlike trustee rights, inherited rights can limited by inherited rights masks. Usually, your effective rights in a directory are the same as your inherited rights for the directory, because masks are rarely set to filter rights. But if you want to be sure, you need to check the directory's inherited rights mask to see if it filters your inherited rights. To do so, complete the following steps.

1. Go to the directory whose mask you want to check.

2. Type

   ALLOW .

The inherited rights mask for the directory is shown. The rights it contains are the inherited rights that it allows to be exercised.

Security Attributes

In addition to your effective rights, attributes may affect what you can do with a directory or its files.

Attributes apply to all users, regardless of their effective rights. They are used mainly as a safeguard against mistakes on the part of any user, and may be set at the directory or file level. There are a number of attributes; here I will explain the most common.

Delete—prevents a directory or file from being deleted.

Hidden—prevents a directory or file from showing in DOS directory scans.

Purge—purges directory or file upon deletion.

Read Write/Read Only—applies only to files. Files marked Read Write can be read from and written to; files marked Read Only cannot be changed, only read.

Shareable—applies only to files. Files marked Shareable can be opened by more than one user at a time.

To see a directory's attributes, go to the directory and type

FLAG

To see a file's attributes, go to the directory which contains the file and type

FLAG *filename*

Moving Up and Down the Directory Tree

Explains how to move up and down the levels of the directory tree with the CD command.

Now you are ready to learn how to move around the directory structure. The following table summarizes how to move up and down in the directory structure. Practice using these commands until you feel comfortable.

Type this ...	... to do this
CD ..	Move up one directory level.
CD ...	Move up two directory levels.
CD	Move up three directory levels.
CD *subdirectory*	Move down one directory level. (If you need to see your current directory's subdirectories, type LISTDIR.)
CD *subdirectory\subdirectory*	Move down two directory levels.

You can customize this section by adding actual directory names to the general instructions given here. You can even delete the general instructions given here and create directions specifically tailored to your directory structure. This would take some effort, but if you have novice users who need a lot of hand-holding, it might be a good idea. On the other hand, if your directory structure changes frequently, it is probably better not to get too specific.

Drive Mappings

> Explains drive mappings.

Drive mappings provide another way to move around in the directory structure. Here is how they work.

Drive mappings point to a particular place in a file server's directory structure. A drive letter is assigned ("mapped") to a directory path, like this:

Drive F: = SERVER\VOLUME:DIRECTORY

Use drive mappings to go directly to a specific point in the directory structure. Type the drive letter, followed by a colon, and press ENTER. In the preceding example, you could go to SERVER\VOLUME:DIRECTORY by typing

F:

Usually, drives are mapped to the areas in the directory structure that you work with most. To see your drive mappings, type

MAP

The mappings are displayed similar to the following:

Drive A: maps to a local disk.
Drive B: maps to a local disk.
Drive C: maps to a local disk.
Drive D: maps to a local disk.
Drive F: = SERVER\VOLUME: \
Drive G: = SERVER\VOLUME:HOME\CHRIS
————————

SEARCH1: = Z:. [SERVER\VOLUME: \PUBLIC]
SEARCH2: = Y:. [SERVER\VOLUME: \]
SEARCH3: = X:. [SERVER\VOLUME: \WORDPROCESSOR]

To customize the preceding section to show the user's actual drive mappings,

1. Delete the example given in the text here, and delete "similar to this" in the sentence that introduces the example.

2. Log in as the user.

3. Go to a directory where the user has the Create right.

4. Type

    MAP >MAPPINGS

5. Retrieve the file MAPPINGS into the text here (SHIFT + F10, MAP-PINGS).

6. Delete extraneous characters and fix spacing as necessary. If you customize this section to show the user's actual mappings, you should also explain the mappings. Sample text that you can use as a starting point is given next.

Here are your drive mappings and what they mean.

Drive	Maps to
A-E	Your PC's floppy and hard disk drives. NetWare security does not apply to these drives. (You can re-map these drives to network drives if desired.)
F	The root directory of volume <VOLUME NAME>.
G	Your personal (home) directory. This is where you keep your personal files. You have all security privileges here—you may create, delete, and rename files and directories, and assign security here.

> Note that both drive and search drive mappings are shown when mappings are listed. Most users won't really need to know about search drive mappings; if you don't want to teach your users about them, you may want to point out the search drive mappings briefly and tell users not to worry about them. If you do want to teach your users about search drive mappings, use the material given next.

Search Drive Mappings

Explains search drive mappings (only necessary for advanced users).

Like drive mappings, search drive mappings point to a location in the file server's directory structure. But search drives work a little differently; they tell the network where to look for a file when it cannot be found in the current directory. The main purpose of search drive mappings is to point to directories that contain executable files (programs you can run), thus preventing you from having to put copies of those files in every directory where you need to work. (Users familiar with DOS recognize that search drives are similar to the PATH command.)

Search drive mappings have both numbers and letters. The numbers begin with one and increase sequentially (2, 3, 4, on up to 16); the letters begin with Z and continue backwards through the alphabet (Y, X, W, and so on).

To see your search drive mappings, type

MAP

Search drive mappings are shown in the lower half of the display.

At this point, you may want to explain what users' specific search drive mappings are used for.

For example, most users should have a search drive mapping to SYS:PUBLIC, that contains the NetWare utilities. To explain this mapping, you would tell them that this is the search drive mapping that points to where the NetWare utilities are located.

Generally, users also have search drive mappings to directories that contain application files. You can explain these mappings too. If you do, this may be a good place to tell users about the applications they will be using on the network.

Sample text that you can use as a starting point is given next.

Here are your search drive mappings and what they mean.

SEARCH1   The file server's PUBLIC directory, where all the NetWare utilities are located. This search mapping allows you to access the NetWare utilities.

SEARCH2   The file server's <insert the directory name> directory, that contains the <insert a description> files. This search mapping allows you to access <utility files, application files, etc.>. You can <describe what their security privileges allow them to do—usually just run files> in this directory.

Looking at Files

Vital for most users.

NetWare gives you many powerful options for listing files. You can limit or sort file listings based on a number of different criteria. The following section summarizes some of the most common options for listing and sorting files.

Type ...	... to see
DIR	Files and directories; file size and last update; directory creation date and time
DIR /W	Files and directories, listed in columns across the screen
NDIR .	Files, file size, last modified date and time, attributes, and owners; directories, inherited rights mask, your effective rights in the directory, owner, and creation date and time
NDIR ACCESS BEF = *mm-dd-yy*	Directories and files that were last accessed before the date specified in the command
NDIR ACCESS AFT = *mm-dd-yy*	Directories and files that were last accessed after the date specified in the command
NDIR UPDATE BEF = *mm-dd-yy*	Directories and files that were last updated before the date specified in the command

NDIR UPDATE AFT = *mm-dd-yy*	Directories and files that were last updated after the date specified in the command
NDIR OWNER=*your username*	Files and directories that you have created
NDIR SORT SIZE	Files sorted by size, smallest to largest
NDIR SORT ACCESS	Files sorted by last access date, earliest to latest
NDIR SORT UPDATE	Files sorted by last update, earliest to latest

Copying Files

Files can be copied with the DOS COPY or the NetWare NCOPY command. I recommend NCOPY, because it is faster. The following section summarizes some of the most common variations of the NCOPY command.

The following instructions assume that users know what source and target directories are, and how to use wildcards. If you have novice users, you may wish to include the following explanation.

Here is an explanation of some terms used in the following explanations:

Source directory—the directory you are copying a file from

Target directory—the directory you are copying a file to

Wildcards—an asterisk (*) that can be used to substitute for other characters in a filename. For example, you can specify all files beginning with "F" by typing

F*

Type ...	**... to**
NCOPY *filename target directory*	Copy a file from your current directory to another directory
NCOPY * *target directory*	Copy all the files in your current directory to another directory. For example, to copy all the files from floppy disk A, type NCOPY A:*.* *target directory*
NCOPY **pattern target directory*	Copy only files that match the pattern from your current directory to another directory. For example, to copy all the files beginning with F, type NCOPY f* *target directory*

If your users have existing files on floppy diskettes, right now might be a good time to have them copy those files from the diskettes to the network.

On the other hand, if you expect your users to create their own directory structures, you may want to wait until after they have done so before they copy their files to the network.

Deleting and Renaming Files

From time to time, you should "clean up" and reorganize your files. That is when you need to know how to delete and rename them. The DOS DEL, ERASE, and REN commands are used to do this.

Type ...	**... to**
DEL *filename* or ERASE *filename*	Delete a file in your current directory
DEL *path:filename* or ERASE *path:filename*	Delete a file that is not in your current directory
REN *filename newname*	Rename a file in your current directory
REN *path:filename newname*	Rename a file that is not in your current directory

Backing Up and Restoring Files

> You may want to substitute a short explanation of your backup policy for the generic paragraph below. And, if you have diskless workstations or do not require users to back up their files, delete this section entirely.

Even though we back up network files regularly, you should still back up your personal files. You needn't back up all your files every day; just back up the ones you have modified that day.

> Explain the best way to back up files on your system. For most users, the simplest thing to do is to back up to a floppy diskette as explained here.

> But if you have users on diskless workstations, or if you are concerned about confidential information floating around on floppy diskettes, you may want to have them back up to another medium.

To back up a file, copy it to a floppy diskette by typing

NCOPY *filename targetpath*

Then, should you need to restore from the backup, you can do so by copying the backup file to its original location.

Salvaging Files

You may or may not want to teach users how to salvage files. It is a great feature and can save a lot of anxiety. But users should rarely have to use it, so you may just want to tell them that it is there and that if they need it, to contact their supervisor.

Sometimes you may delete or lose a file accidentally in spite of all your precautions. If this happens, all may not be lost. Often, you can salvage the file from the file server's hard disk using the SALVAGE menu utility.

SALVAGE works because there are two steps in deleting a file. The first is to mark it for deletion. (This is what you are actually doing when you delete a file with DELETE or ERASE.) Files marked for deletion actually stay on the hard disk until they are purged (permanently deleted), or the space they occupy is needed by other files. That is why you can often salvage an erased file by completing the following steps:

1. Access SALVAGE.

2. Go to the directory you want to salvage the files from, if it is not your current directory.

   NOTE: Files must be salvaged from the directory they were in when they were deleted. If you deleted the directory as well as the files, your files can still be salvaged. However, the supervisor will have to help you. (If a file's directory is deleted, the file is saved in special directory called DELETED.SAV. Since many users could have files in this directory, most users do not have rights to salvage from it.)

   a. Choose "Select Current Directory."

b. Backspace to delete the parts of the path you do not want.

c. If you know the path, type it in. If you do not, press Insert and choose directories til you get to where you want.

d. Press Escape.

e. Press Enter.

Your current directory should be shown at the top of the screen, in the header.

3. To sort the recoverable files based on certain criteria, specify the criteria.

a. Choose "Set Salvage Options."

b. Choose the menu option you want to sort the files based on.

4. Now you are ready to view the recoverable files.

a. Choose "View/Recover Deleted Files."

b. To see only files which match a certain pattern, specify the pattern.

c. Press Enter.

You see a list of all recoverable files, sorted as you specified.

d. Choose the file(s) you wish to recover.

To choose more than one, mark each with the F5 key.

e. Answer "Yes."

The files are recovered to their original directory.

Purging Files

PURGE is a potentially dangerous command for users to know about. Users can only purge files they can delete, so they can not do more damage than their security allows. On the other hand, they may purge a file or files that they will want to recover later.

It is up to you if you want to teach your users about PURGE, of course. It all depends on how much responsibility you want to give them.

Purging a file erases it for good; purged files cannot be recovered. Reasonably enough, you can not purge files which your security does not allow you to delete.

There are a couple of reasons to purge files. The first is if they contain sensitive information and you want to get rid of them for good. The second is if you want to keep the disk really clean.

The following table summarizes how to purge files.

Type this ...	.. to do this
PURGE *filename*	Purge a file in your current directory
PURGE *path:filename*	Purge a file not in your current directory
PURGE *.*	Purge all the files in a directory
PURGE ALL	Purge all recoverable files

Printing Files

If you use a third-party printing program on your network, you may want to substitute instructions for using that printing program for the NetWare printing instructions given here.

Generally, I do not recommend that you teach users how to print their files with NetWare. This is why.

- For most users, it is much easier to print using applications. If you set up network printing properly and test it thoroughly, printing from applications should be transparent to users.

- NetWare printing is complex, and users need to understand it fairly well to be comfortable with the NetWare printing utilities. Generally, it makes more sense to set up custom menus for users to print from than to educate users about the many printing parameters.

- If users need to print with CAPTURE, it makes more sense to include the CAPTURE TI=n command in their login scripts or a batch file than to try and teach them how CAPTURE works (see the explanation of CAPTURE in Chapter 6, "Command Line Utilities Reference"). However, if you do wish to teach your users how to print from the command line, you can include this short explanation of NetWare printing and the NPRINT command in their manuals.

Printing on a network is a little more involved than printing with a regular personal computer. Instead of going directly from your personal computer to the printer, print data must follow a somewhat more complex path. This path was set up when the network was installed, so you shouldn't have to worry about it. But briefly, it is as follows on the next page.

First, the print data ("print job" in NetWare terms) goes to a network print queue located on the file server's hard disk. Like the personal computer's buffer or spool area, the print queue is a waiting area for print jobs that pile up faster than they can be printed. However, a network print queue stores jobs from many different users. Which queue your print jobs go to depends on how network printing has been set up, or which queue you specify when you print the job.

> You may wish to tell them which print queue(s) their print jobs go to, and why, here.

A process called a print server takes print jobs out of the queue and sends them to the printer. As with print queues, print servers are established when network printing is set up. Which queues a print server services, and which printers it sends print jobs to, depends on how network printing was set up.

> You may wish to tell them which printer(s) their print jobs go to, and why, here.

Luckily, you do not really need to know all this information to print a file. If the file was created in a network application or text editor, just print it from there. If the file was created in a non-network application or text editor, you can print it with NPRINT. The following section summarizes how this is done.

Type ...	... to
NPRINT *filename*	Print a file created in a non-network application or text editor
NPRINT *filename* NOTI	Be notified when the job has printed
NPRINT *filename* C=*n*	Print a certain number of copies (replace *n* with the desired number)

Working with Directories

Most of the time, when you clean up and reorganize, you work with files. But sometimes you also work with the directory structure itself.

The following section summarizes how to list, create, rename, and delete directories, as well as how to copy directory structures.

Type ...	... to
LISTDIR	List your current directory's subdirectories
MD *directory*	Create a subdirectory beneath your current directory
RENDIR *directory newname*	Rename a subdirectory of your current directory
RD *directory*	Delete a subdirectory of your current directory (the subdirectory must be completely empty before you can delete it)
NCOPY . /S /E *target directory*	Copy the entire subdirectory tree beneath your current directory to another location. (The /S flag copies the subdirectories; the /E flag copies subdirectories even if they are empty.)

Ideas for Creating Your Own Directory Structures

Include if user

- Is sophisticated enough to organize his or her files in directories

- Has the Create right at any point in the directory structure (necessary to create directories)

The directory structure for the file server organizes files for everyone who works on the file server. In the areas where you keep your own personal files, you may wish to create your own small directory structures to organize your files. In fact, if you have more than a few files, this is a good idea: you should not dump your electronic files onto a computer without organizing them any more than you would dump your paper files onto a desk or into a drawer.

As you plan your directory structure, consider these questions.

1. What will I organize my files based on?

   Consider what files you have to manage, and what kind of structure would help you best organize them. It may be useful to think of how you would organize ordinary paper files efficiently, and use that as a guideline for planning your directory structure.

2. Do other people need to access my files?

   If so, it may make sense to put files that need to be accessed by the same people in the same directories.

3. What should I name my directories?

    Give your directories meaningful, descriptive names.

4. How many levels deep should I make my directory structure?

    Generally, it is best not to make the directory structure more than 3-4 levels deep.

    If you start getting a lot of files in a directory, consider subdividing the directory and reorganizing your files.

Once you have decided how you want to organize your personal directory structures, use the DOS MD command to create directories according to your plan.

Creating a Directory

To create a directory,

1. Move to the directory that you would like to create the new directory beneath.

2. Type

MD *directory*

Substitute the name of your new directory for directory. Remember, it can only be eight characters long; if you type a longer name, it is truncated to eight characters.

Setting Up Drive Mappings

Most users probably won't need to see drive mappings, and even fewer need to set up search drive mappings. The main reason to set up a search drive mapping is if the user uses personal applications on the network.

In addition, drive and search drive mappings consume directory entries. If you are concerned about excessive drive mappings consuming directory entries, you may not want to teach your users how to set up mappings.

Also, if you did not include the previous sections explaining drive and search drive mappings, you won't want to include this section either.

You probably won't need to set up drive mappings to your newly-created subdirectories unless your subdirectory structure is quite deep and complex. In most cases, it is easier to use your existing drive mappings to get to the general area, then move up and down the directory structure. But if you do want to set up drive mappings, here is how to do it.

Type

MAP *driveletter*:=*path*

Substitute the next available letter for *driveletter*; substitute the desired directory path for *path*. If you need to see which drive letter is the next one available, type MAP to check your existing drive mappings.

Saving Mappings in Login Scripts

This section explains how to save mappings in personal login scripts. If you teach users how to save drive mappings in their login scripts, caution them not to override the system login script mappings.

Drive mappings set up at the command line last only until you log out. Most of the time, you want your drive mappings to be more permanent than that. To have your drive mappings set up every time you log in, you must save them in your login script. To do so, complete the following steps.

1. Access the SYSCON utility.

2. Choose "User Information."

3. Choose your name.

4. Choose Login Script.

    You see your login script. It may have many or few commands. Be very careful when you are working in the login script. Make sure you understand the intent of each line before you make any changes.

5. To set the drive mapping, type

    MAP *n:=*directory path*

6. Exit SYSCON, saving your changes.

Now login again. Type MAP to display your drive mappings (if they are not shown when you login). You should see the drive mappings you added.

Setting Security

> Setting security is a fairly advanced topic that most users won't really be concerned with. If you have set up the high-level directory structure properly, users should not have to worry about other users accessing their personal files. Some users may create files in their personal directories that they share with other users; these are probably the only users who might be concerned with setting security.
>
> Remember, unless a user has the Supervisory or Access Control right in a directory, he or she cannot set security anyway. So skip this section for all users who do not have these rights anywhere.
>
> Also, if you include this section, make sure you included the full explanation of security previously, since users need to understand inherited rights masks and trustee rights before they set security.

In the directories where you have the Supervisory or Access Control right, you can set security if you wish. Unless you create directories or files which you need to share with other users, you probably won't need to do this, however.

If you do need to assign security, follow these steps.

1. Decide which users need which rights in your directories.

   You may want to sketch the directory tree and write in the names of users who need access to certain directories, along with what rights they should be given. Remember, once you have granted a trustee right in a directory, the right trickles down the tree. So you may not need to actually make trustee assignments in every single directory where you want the user to have security privileges.

You may also want to refer to the following rights table as you decide what rights to grant.

Letter	Right	Lets you ...
S	Supervisory	Exercise all rights for directory or file
R	Read	Directory level: Open a directory's files and read them or copy them to other directories
		File level: Open a file and read it or copy it to another directory
W	Write	Directory level: Change contents of files in directory
		File level: Change contents of file
C	Create	Directory level: Create files and subdirectories
		File level: Salvage deleted files; create and write a file
E	Erase	Directory level: Delete empty directories
		File level: Delete the file
M	Modify	Directory level: Change directory attributes; rename subdirectories and files
		File level: Change the file's attributes; re-name the file
F	File Scan	Directory level: See files and subdirectories
		File level: See the file
A	Access Control	Assign security for directory or file

2. Decide if you want to limit the rights that users can inherit into any given directory.

   Sometimes, you want to be sure that a certain right cannot be inherited into a given directory. For example, you may want to make sure that no one can inherit the Erase right into a given directory. When this is the case, you should set the directory's inherited rights mask so the directory masks the right.

   Remember, an inherited rights mask blocks users' inherited rights only for the directory to which the mask is assigned.

   If you sketched the directory tree, write in the inherited rights masks on your sketch.

3. Check to be sure that the trustee assignments and inherited rights masks that you have planned give users the rights you want them to have in your directories.

4. Make trustee assignments.

   For each directory where you wish to make a trustee assignment, go to the directory and type

   > GRANT *rights* TO *username*

   Replace *rights* with the abbreviations for the desired rights, with a space between each right; replace *username* with the name of the user you are giving the rights to.

For example, to grant user Mark Read, Open, and Search rights in a directory, you would go to that directory and type

GRANT R O S TO MARK

Complete the above steps for every trustee assignment you want to make. Remember that trustee rights trickle down through the directory structure, so you needn't make a trustee assignment in every directory where you want a user to have rights.

5. Change inherited rights masks if necessary.

For each directory whose inherited rights mask you wish to change, go to the directory and type

ALLOW *rights*

Replace *rights* with the rights you wish the mask to allow, with a space between each right.

For example, to have a directory's inherited rights mask allow all rights except the Supervisory right, you would go to the directory and type

ALLOW R W C E M F A

Conclusion

The following generic conclusion is based on the unmodified Manual Maker text for this chapter. Modify it based on how you modified the chapter.

In this chapter, you learned about

- Directory structures, directory paths, and directory names

- NetWare security and how it controls what you can do on the network

- Moving around the directory tree with the CD command and drive mappings

- Working with files, including listing, copying, deleting, renaming, backing up and restoring, printing, salvaging and purging

- Working with directories, including listing, creating, copying, deleting, and renaming

- Setting up your own drive mappings

- Establishing security in your personal areas of the directory structure

Working with Directories and Files (Menu Utilities Version)

This boilerplate chapter is found in
FILESMEN.WP (WordPerfect version)
FILESMEN.ASC (ASCII version)

CHAPTER 5

Working with Directories and Files

Menu Utilities Version

This chapter explains how to work with directories and files. It explains concepts, such as how directory structures and drive mappings work; and how to complete basic tasks, such as creating directories, copying files, and deleting files.

As with the rest of the Manual Maker, the approach you take in this chapter depends on how you have set up your network, how experienced your users are, and how much you want to teach them.

Directory Structures

This section explains directory structures and how they work.

A network contains a lot of information. Without some sort of organization, that information is very difficult to work with. But rest assured, there is an effective way to organize network information.

The information on a file server's hard disk is organized by the file server's directory structure, a type of electronic filing system. A directory structure is made up of directories, areas of the hard disk that contain files and other directories. Directories are placed inside other directories, forming a branching, tree-like structure. (In fact, directory structures are often called directory trees.) Files are then organized by placing them inside the directory structure.

Directories have special names that describe their relationship to each other in the structure:

A **volume**, the highest level in the structure, is an actual physical area on the hard disk. All directories are subdivisions of the volume.

The **root directory** is the volume level. The root directory is designated by a backslash (\). It contains all of the other directories on the volume.

A directory's **parent directory** is the directory immediately above the directory.

The current, or **default**, directory is your current location in the directory structure. NetWare and DOS both look for data and program files in this directory first. If another directory isn't specified, this directory is assumed.

A **subdirectory** of a directory is any directory located below that directory.

A Sample Directory Structure

Here is part of a sample directory structure. The levels in this structure are labeled in parentheses at the bottom of the diagram.

> If you want to substitute an actual directory structure from your server, go ahead. I used this one because it corresponds closely to how many users' home directories are set up.
>
> If you use an actual directory structure in this example, use the same directory structure in the next example too.

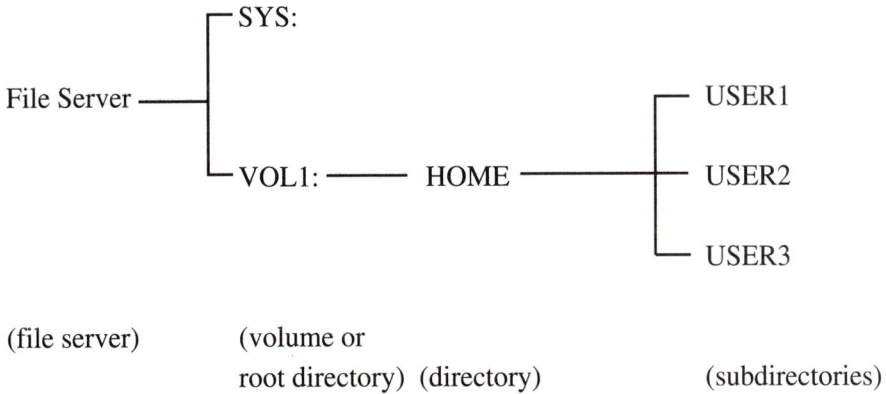

```
                    ┌─ SYS:
File Server ────────┤
                    └─ VOL1: ───── HOME ───────┬─ USER1
                                               ├─ USER2
                                               └─ USER3

   (file server)        (volume or
                         root directory)  (directory)        (subdirectories)
```

Directory Paths

This section explains directory paths and directory names.

To find a file, you must know where it is located in the directory structure. A file's location is indicated by its directory path, or "path" for short. The path consists of the file server, volume, root directory, and any other directories leading up to the file.

Here is the same directory structure you saw before, with a directory path indicated by asterisks.

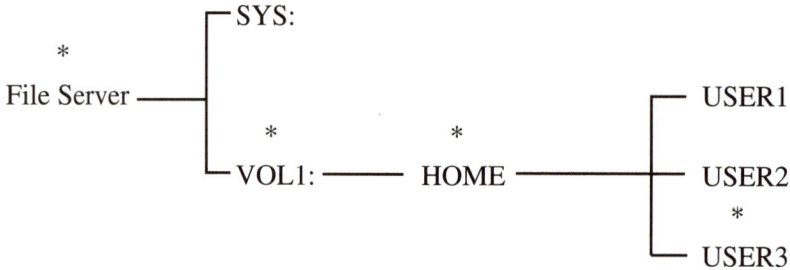

The path indicated by the asterisks would be specified as follows:

FILESERVER\VOL1:HOME\USER3

Exploring the Directory Tree

Now that you understand what directory structures are and how they work, let's explore the part of the directory tree where you can work. To do so, complete these steps.

1. Access FILER.

2. Choose "Select Current Directory."

   In the box that appears, you'll see the directory path for your current directory, something like this:

   FILESERVER/VOLUME:DIRECTORY

3. To move UP a level or levels, use the backspace key to delete parts of the path. In the example on the preceding page, you could move up to the volume level by deleting the directory so the path looked like this:

   FILESERVER/VOLUME:

   You can also move up a level by choosing the ".." option to go to the directory's parent directory.

4. To move DOWN a level, you can type the desired path. Or you can press INSERT to list the directory's subdirectories, then choose the directory you want.

   When you've specified the path you want, press ESCAPE, then ENTER. The center of the header will now show your new directory path, which is now your current directory.

   NOTE: You may get a message telling you that you have no search rights for a directory. If so, just press ESCAPE to make the message go away.

Drive Mappings

> Explains the concept of drive mappings.

Drive mappings give you another way to move around in the directory structure. Here's how they work.

Drive mappings point to a particular place in a file server's directory structure. A drive letter is assigned ("mapped") to a directory path, like this:

Drive F: = SERVER\VOLUME:DIRECTORY

Usually, drives are mapped to the areas in the directory structure that you will work with a lot. To see your drive mappings,

1. Access SESSION.

2. Choose "Drive Mappings" and your drive mappings will be listed.

   You'll probably recognize the directories shown in your mappings; they are most likely the same directories you've just been exploring.

   You can use drive mappings to go directly to a specific point in the directory structure. To move directly to a directory which is mapped to a given drive,

3. Press ESCAPE to return to the SESSION Available Topics menu.

4. Choose "Select Default Drive."

5. Choose the drive you want to be your current (default) drive. The directory it is mapped to will then become your current directory.

Search Drive Mappings

> Explains the concept of search drive mappings. Probably only necessary for advanced users.

Like drive mappings, search drive mappings point to a location in the file server's directory structure. But search drives work a little differently; they tell the network where to look for a file when it can't be found in the current directory. The main purpose of search drive mappings is to point to directories which contain executable files (programs you can run), thus preventing you from having to put copies of those files in every directory where you need to work. (Users familiar with DOS will recognize that search drives are similar to the PATH command.) Usually, search drives are mapped to the areas in the directory structure that contain the executable files you need to use.

Search drive mappings have both numbers and letters. The numbers begin with one and increase (2, 3, 4, and so on); the letters begin with Z and continue up the alphabet (Y, X, W, and so on).

To see your search drive mappings,

1. Access SESSION.

2. Choose "Search Mappings" and your search drive mappings will be listed.

Approaches to NetWare Security

Network security is a fairly complex topic, and there are many possible approaches to it. In this section, I've offered you three. I recommend that you skim through all the explanations before deciding which approach to take. Then pick the one that comes closest to what you want, and modify as desired.

Network Security, Approach #1: Basic

This approach allows you to skirt the issue of security almost entirely. You simply tell users where they can work and what they can do. It's a bottom-line approach that does not even deal with the actual details of security, but simply explains the end results from a user's perspective. I recommend this approach for novice users.

If you choose this approach,

- Set up your security very carefully so that users won't run into problems.

- Test your security by logging in as the user and making sure that you can do everything you want the user to be able to do.

- Realize that the burden of troubleshooting security-related problems (that account for many common network problems) rests squarely on you, as supervisor.

Network Security

Network security determines what directories and files you can access on our network, and what you can do with those directories and files.

Here are the directories you can work with on our network and what you can do in each directory.

List the directories where the users have security privileges (rights), and indicate what the user can do in each directory, based on what his or her rights are. You can do this as follows:

1. Log in as the user.

2. Move to a directory where the user has the Create right.

3. Type CLS to clear the screen.

4. At the DOS prompt, type
   WHOAMI /R >MYRIGHTS

5. Now retrieve the file MYRIGHTS into this document and remove any extraneous information.

6. Delete the file MYRIGHTS from the directory where you created it.

If you customize the preceding example, you should also explain it. The following example walks you through the process of customizing the example for user Diana, and gives you ideas and sample explanations. (Because the example is lengthy, I haven't put it into comments. You should delete most of this explanation from your user manuals, of course. However, you may want to modify portions of it for use in your manuals.)

To modify this Security section for user Diana, I would complete these steps.

1. Log in as Diana.

2. Move to Diana's personal directory, SYS:HOME\DIANA.

3. Type CLS.

4. Type

   WHOAMI /R >MYRIGHTS

5. Move to the appropriate place in this document.

6. Retrieve the file MYRIGHTS into this document (SHIFT F10, \HOME\DIANA\MYRIGHTS).

   At this point, MYRIGHTS looks something like the following:

^^ ^P ^— ^Q ^^ ^PYou are user DIANA attached to server LATE, connection 1.
Server LATE is running NetWare 386 V3.10 Rev. A.
Login time: Monday October 15, 1990 10:40 am
```
   [        ]           SYS:
    [ R      F ]        SYS:LOGIN
    [ R      F ]        SYS:PUBLIC
    [    C   ]          SYS:MAIL
    [ RWCEMF ]          SYS:MAIL/4000001
     [ RWCEMFA]         SYS:HOME/DIANA
 [    R       F ]       SYS:WP51
```

7. Remove the extraneous characters and fix the spacing so that MYRIGHTS looks like this:

```
[           ]        SYS:
[ R       F ]        SYS:LOGIN
[ R       F ]        SYS:PUBLIC
[    C    ]          SYS:MAIL
[ RWCEMF ]           SYS:MAIL/4000001
[SRWCEMFA]           SYS:HOME/DIANA
[ R       F ]        SYS:WP51
```

8. Add explanations.

You may want to comment on how the tree is organized and why it is organized that way. For example,

A. Give a general explanation of each directory's purpose. (You may wish to delete the directories that you do not want to tell the user about—for example most users do not need to know about directories such as SYS:LOGIN, SYS:PUBLIC, and SYS:MAIL.)

B. Mention which directories contain applications and utilities, and which contain data files.

C. Point out the user's home directory, if you have created one.

D. Explain which directories contain shared files, such as database files, and tell who else has access to such directories.

You should also tell the user what he or can do in each directory (create files, look at files, organize a structure beneath, etc.). Use the rights sets as your guide.

With explanations, the MYRIGHTS file now looks like this:

[SRWCEMFA] SYS:DIANA This is your personal directory. You have all security privileges here. You can list, create, delete, and modify files; create, delete, and rename directories; and assign security.

[R   F] SYS:WP51 This directory contains the WordPerfect application files. Your security privileges allow you to run these files, but nothing else.

9. Delete the rights sets and adjust the spacing. After this step, the sample file MYRIGHTS looks similar to this (notice that I have not included explanations for all of the directories where the user has rights):

SYS:DIANA This is your personal directory. You have all security privileges here. You can list, create, delete, and modify files; create, delete, and rename directories; and assign security.

SYS:WP51 This directory contains the WordPerfect application files. Your security privileges allow you to run these files, but nothing else.

Network Security, Approach #2: Intermediate

This approach deals briefly with security, explaining everything that most non-administrative users need to know. It is a middle-of-the road approach that covers only effective rights and how they determine what a user can do with a directory or file. I recommend it for most intermediate users.

If you choose this approach, you should still set up and test your security carefully. If security problems do come up, you will probably still have to help users, since they can not change their own security. But even so, I think it is worth teaching users a little about security, because many common problems are security-related (for example, not being able to run an application.)

NetWare Security

Network security determines what directories and files you can access on our network, and what you can do with those directories and files.

Your network security is based on the security privileges that you are allowed to exercise in any given directory or for any given file. These are called your "effective rights." There are eight rights shown between brackets, like this:

[SRWCEMFA]

Each letter stands for a right that allows certain privileges, as summarized in the following table. Notice that sometimes the meaning of a right varies depending on what level it applies to (directory or file).

Letter	Right	Lets you ...
S	Supervisory	Exercise all rights for directory or file
R	Read	Directory level: Open a directory's files and read them or copy them to other directories
		File level: Open a file and read it or copy it to another directory
W	Write	Directory level: Change contents of files in directory
		File level: Change contents of file
C	Create	Directory level: Create files and subdirectories
		File level: Salvage deleted files; create and write a file
E	Erase	Directory level: Delete empty directories
		File level: Delete the file
M	Modify	Directory level: Change directory attributes; rename subdirectories and files
		File level: Change the file's attributes; re-name the file
F	File Scan	Directory level: See files and subdirectories
		File level: See the file
A	Access Control	Assign security for directory or file

Unfortunately, no NetWare Menu utility will give a user an overview of his or her effective rights throughout the entire directory structure. A user can see all of his or her trustee assignments (in SYSCON), but effective rights must be reviewed directory by directory (in FILER).

For this reason, I recommend that you tell users which directories they have rights to work with, and what their effective rights are in those directories. The following example walks you through the process of doing so for user Diana, and gives you ideas and sample explanations. (Because the example is lengthy, I haven't put it into comments. You'll want to delete most of this explanation from your users' manuals, of course. However, you may want to modify portions of it for use in your manuals.)

If you don't want to be this detailed in individual user manuals, delete this section and just tell users how to see their effective rights.

Example: Customizing the Security Section

To modify this security section for user Diana, I would complete these steps.

1. Log in as Diana.

2. Move to Diana's personal directory, SYS:HOME\DIANA.

3. Type CLS.

4. Type

    WHOAMI /R >MYRIGHTS

5. Move to the appropriate place in this document.

6. Retrieve the file MYRIGHTS into this document (SHIFT F10, \HOME\DIANA\MYRIGHTS).

At this point, MYRIGHTS looks something like this:

^^ ^P ^— ^Q ^^ ^PYou are user DIANA attached to server LATE, connection 1.
Server LATE is running NetWare 386 V3.10 Rev. A.
Login time: Monday October 15, 1990 10:40 am

```
[          ]          SYS:
 [ R      F ]          SYS:LOGIN
  [ R      F ]          SYS:PUBLIC
  [    C    ]          SYS:MAIL
  [ RWCEMF ]          SYS:MAIL/4000001
    [ RWCEMFA]          SYS:HOME/DIANA
  [ R         F ]          SYS:WP51
```

7. Remove the extraneous characters and fix the spacing so that MYRIGHTS looks like this:

```
[          ]          SYS:
[ R      F ]          SYS:LOGIN
[ R      F ]          SYS:PUBLIC
[    C    ]          SYS:MAIL
[ RWCEMF  ]          SYS:MAIL/4000001
[SRWCEMFA]          SYS:HOME/DIANA
[ R         F ]          SYS:WP51
```

8. Add explanations.

You may want to comment on how the tree is organized and why it is organized that way. For example,

A. Give a general explanation of each directory's purpose. (You may wish to delete the directories that you do not want to tell the user about—for example most users do not need to know about directories such as SYS:LOGIN, SYS:PUBLIC, and SYS:MAIL.)

B. Mention which directories contain applications and utilities, and which contain data files.

C. Point out the user's home directory, if you have created one.

D. Explain which directories contain shared files, such as database files, and tell who else has access to such directories.

You should also tell the user what he or can do in each directory (create files, look at files, organize a structure beneath, etc.). Use the rights sets as your guide as you do this.

With explanations, MYRIGHTS looks something like this:

[   ]   Diana has no rights in the SYS directory.

[R   F]   Diana has Read and File Scan rights in three directories, LOGIN, PUBLIC, and WP51. Read allows Diana to open files and read their contents of files, and File Scan allows her to list the files. This combination of rights lets Diana run executable (program) files, which these directories contain. She does not have any other rights because she should not be able to delete, rename, or otherwise modify these files.

[RWCEMF]   Diana has all rights but Supervisory and Access Control in a directory beneath the MAIL directory, which is assigned to her.

[C   ]   Diana has the Create right in the MAIL directory. This creates a "drop-box" directory, where Diana can only create files. The files created in this directory have to do with the NetWare electronic mail system.

[SRWCEMFA]   Diana has all rights in her home directory (DIANA), and the directories beneath it (MYM and WORDPROC). Thus, she has all privileges here.

Checking Your Effective Rights for Individual Directories or Files

To see your effective rights for a directory, complete these steps.

1. Access FILER.

2. Go to the directory where you wish to see your effective rights.

3. Choose "Current Directory Information."

   Your effective rights will be displayed in the resulting screen.

To see your effective rights for a file, complete these steps.

1. Access FILER.

2. Go to the directory which contains the file for which you wish to see your effective rights.

3. Choose "Directory Contents."

4. Choose the file.

5. Choose "View/Set File Information."

   Your effective rights will be displayed in the resulting screen.

Network Security, Approach #3: Advanced

This approach offers a complete explanation of security, including effective rights, trustee rights, inherited rights masks, and attributes. Security can get fairly involved at this level, so I do not recommend this approach for many users; for most users, it is sufficient—and simpler—to just see their effective rights. However, you might want to take this approach if you have advanced users and

- You have given them the Supervisory or Access Control right in some directories and expect them to assign security in those directories

- You want to train them to be as independent as possible

- You expect them to troubleshoot

NetWare Security

Network security determines what directories and files you can access on our network, and what you can do with those directories and files.

Your network security is based on the security privileges you are allowed to exercise in any given directory or for any given file. These are called your "effective rights." There are eight rights, shown here between brackets:

[SRWCEMFA]

Each letter stands for a right that allows certain privileges, as summarized in the following table. Notice that sometimes the meaning of a right varies depending on what level it has been assigned at (directory or file).

Letter	Right	Lets you ...
S	Supervisory	Exercise all rights for directory or file
R	Read	Directory level: Open a directory's files and read them or copy them to other directories
		File level: Open a file and read it or copy it to another directory
W	Write	Directory level: Change contents of files in directory
		File level: Change contents of file
C	Create	Directory level: Create files and subdirectories
		File level: Salvage deleted files; create and write a file
E	Erase	Directory level: Delete empty directories
		File level: Delete the file
M	Modify	Directory level: Change directory attributes; rename subdirectories and files
		File level: Change the file's attributes; re-name the file
F	File Scan	Directory level: See files and subdirectories
		File level: See the file
A	Access Control	Assign security for directory or file

Unfortunately, no NetWare Menu utility will give a user an overview of his or her effective rights throughout the entire directory structure. A user can see all of his or her trustee assignments (in SYSCON), but effective rights must be reviewed directory by directory (in FILER).

For this reason, I recommend that you tell users which directories they have rights to work with, and what their effective rights are in those directories. The following example walks you through the process of doing so for user Diana, and gives you ideas and sample explanations. (Because the example is lengthy, I haven't put it into comments. You'll want to delete most of this explanation from your users' manuals, of course. However, you may want to modify portions of it for use in your manuals.)

If you don't want to be this detailed in individual user manuals, delete this section and just tell users how to see their effective rights.

Example: Customizing the Security Section

To modify this security section for user Diana, I would complete these steps.

1. Log in as Diana.

2. Move to Diana's personal directory, SYS:HOME\DIANA.

3. Type CLS.

4. Type

   WHOAMI /R >MYRIGHTS

5. Move to the appropriate place in this document.

6. Retrieve the file MYRIGHTS into this document (SHIFT F10, \HOME\DIANA\MYRIGHTS).

At this point, MYRIGHTS looks something like this:

^^ ^P ^— ^Q ^^ ^PYou are user DIANA attached to server LATE, connection 1.
Server LATE is running NetWare 386 V3.10 Rev. A.
Login time: Monday October 15, 1990 10:40 am

```
[          ]            SYS:
 [ R      F ]           SYS:LOGIN
 [ R      F ]           SYS:PUBLIC
 [    C    ]            SYS:MAIL
 [ RWCEMF  ]            SYS:MAIL/4000001
 [ RWCEMFA]             SYS:HOME/DIANA
 [ R      F ]           SYS:WP51
```

7. Remove the extraneous characters and fix the spacing so that MYRIGHTS looks like this:

```
[          ]            SYS:
[ R      F ]            SYS:LOGIN
[ R      F ]            SYS:PUBLIC
[    C    ]             SYS:MAIL
[ RWCEMF  ]            SYS:MAIL/4000001
[SRWCEMFA]             SYS:HOME/DIANA
[ R      F ]           SYS:WP51
```

8. Add explanations.

You may want to comment on how the tree is organized and why it is organized that way. For example,

A. Give a general explanation of each directory's purpose. (You may wish to delete the directories that you do not want to tell the user about—for example most users do not need to know about directories such as SYS:LOGIN, SYS:PUBLIC, and SYS:MAIL.)

B. Mention which directories contain applications and utilities, and which contain data files.

C. Point out the user's home directory, if you have created one.

D. Explain which directories contain shared files, such as database files, and tell who else has access to such directories.

You should also tell the user what he or can do in each directory (create files, look at files, organize a structure beneath, etc.). Use the rights sets as your guide as you do this.

With explanations, MYRIGHTS looks something like this:

[   ]   Diana has no rights in the SYS directory.

[R   F]   Diana has Read and File Scan rights in three directories, LOGIN, PUBLIC, and WP51. Read allows Diana to open files and read their contents of files, and File Scan allows her to list the files. This combination of rights lets Diana run executable (program) files, which these directories contain. She does not have any other rights because she should not be able to delete, rename, or otherwise modify these files.

[RWCEMF]   Diana has all rights but Supervisory and Access Control in a directory beneath the MAIL directory, which is assigned to her.

[C   ]   Diana has the Create right in the MAIL directory. This creates a "drop-box" directory, where Diana can only create files. The files created in this directory have to do with the NetWare electronic mail system.

[SRWCEMFA]   Diana has all rights in her home directory (DIANA), and the directories beneath it (MYM and WORDPROC). Thus, she has all privileges here.

Checking Your Effective Rights for Individual Directories or Files

To see your effective rights for a directory, complete these steps.

1. Access FILER.

2. Go to the directory where you wish to see your effective rights.

3. Choose "Current Directory Information."

Your effective rights will be displayed in the resulting screen.

To see your effective rights for a file, complete these steps.

1. Access FILER.

2. Go to the directory which contains the file which you wish to see your effective rights for.

3. Choose "Directory Contents."

4. Choose the file.

5. Choose "View/Set File Information."

Your effective rights will be displayed in the resulting screen.

How Your Effective Rights Were Determined

Your effective rights are determined by the rights granted to you as a user (your "trustee rights"), and the rights which a directory allows to be exercised (its "inherited rights mask").

Trustee rights. When you are explicitly given privileges in a directory or file, you are called a "trustee" and your rights are called your "trustee rights." Trustee rights are the main method of authorizing you to work with directories and files.

Trustee rights can be assigned at any level in the directory tree—even at the file level, though this is rare. Usually, trustee assignments are granted at the highest level that is appropriate in a directory structure. When you are given trustee rights for a directory or file, your effective rights for the directory or file are the same as your trustee rights.

You may be given trustee rights directly, as a user. You may also be given trustee rights indirectly, through security equivalences. There are several types of security equivalences: you may be security-equivalent to another user, or you may be a member of a group, which makes you security-equivalent to the group. It is very common to gain the majority of your trustee rights via membership in groups.

Trustee rights "trickle down" through the subdirectory tree beneath the directory where they were granted, giving you the same rights in the subdirectory tree as in the directory. Rights gained by inheritance from a trustee assignment further up the directory tree are called "inherited rights." Inherited rights may be limited by inherited rights masks, as explained next.

Inherited Rights Masks. An inherited rights mask filters all users' inherited rights for a directory or file. Masks prevent users from accidentally inheriting more rights than they should have for a file or directory. Masks are a safeguard, and should rarely be set. The default is for an inherited rights mask to allow all rights.

Inherited rights masks do not filter trustee rights (those explicitly granted in a directory or file). They only filter inherited rights (those which "trickled down" from a trustee assignment granted at a higher level in the directory tree). There is, however, one exception: the Supervisory right is never filtered. If you want to see how your effective rights for a directory or file were determined, you need to know several things:

1. Do you have trustee rights or inherited rights for the directory or file?

2. Does the directory or file's inherited rights mask filter any rights?

Usually, it is sufficient to know this information at the directory level.

Let's start by looking at your trustee assignments.

To see the trustee assignments you have been given in a directory as a user,

1. Access SYSCON.

2. Choose "User Information."

3. Choose your name.

4. Choose "Trustee Directory Assignments."

> You then see the directories where you have been given trustee rights, and what those trustee rights are. These are also your effective rights for the directories, regardless of whether the directories' inherited rights masks filter rights, because inherited rights masks do not filter trustee rights.

To see the trustee assignments you have been given indirectly, via your membership in groups, you first need to know which groups you belong to. To do so,

1. Access SYSCON.

2. Choose "User Information."

3. Choose your name.

4. Choose "Groups Belonged To."

Once you know which groups you belong to, you need to find out what their trustee assignments are. To do so, complete the following steps:

1. Access SYSCON.

2. Choose "Group Information."

3. Choose one of the groups you belong to.

4. Choose "Trustee Directory Assignments."

You then see the directories where the group has been given trustee rights, and what those trustee rights are. These are also the group's effective rights for the directories, regardless of whether the directories' inherited rights masks filter rights, because inherited rights masks do not filter trustee rights. You have the same trustee rights as the group, since you are a member of it.

The trustee rights you have been given in a directory then filter down through its subdirectory tree. These rights are your inherited rights for these subdirectories.

Unlike trustee rights, inherited rights can be limited by inherited rights masks. Usually, your effective rights in a directory are the same as your inherited rights for the directory, because masks are rarely set to filter rights. But if you want to be sure, you need to check the directory's inherited rights mask to see if it filters your inherited rights. To do so, complete these steps.

1. Access FILER.

2. Go to the directory whose mask you wish to see.

3. Choose "Current Directory Information."

The directory's inherited rights mask is shown near the bottom of the screen.

Security Attributes

In addition to your effective rights, attributes may affect what you can do with a directory or its files.

Attributes apply to all users, regardless of their effective rights. They are used mainly as a safeguard against mistakes on the part of any user, and may be set at the directory or file level. There are a number of attributes; here I will explain the most common.

Delete—prevents a directory or file from being deleted.

Hidden—prevents a directory or file from showing in DOS directory scans

Purge—purges directory or file upon deletion

Read Write/Read Only—applies only to files. Files marked Read Write can be read from and written to; files marked Read Only cannot be changed, only read.

Shareable—applies only to files. Files marked Shareable can be opened by more than one user at a time.

To see a directory's attributes, complete these steps.

1. Access FILER.

2. Choose "Current Directory Information."

3. Choose the "(see list)" field next to "Directory Attributes."

To see a file's attributes, complete these steps.

1. Access FILER.

2. Choose "Directory Contents."

3. Choose the file whose attributes you wish to see.

4. Choose "View/Set File Information."

The file's attributes are shown at the top of the screen.

Looking at Files

Vital for almost all users.

To see a directory's files and subdirectories,

1. Access FILER.

2. Choose "Directory Contents."

3. The directory's subdirectories and files will be listed.

   NOTE: You may get a message telling you that you have no search rights for a directory. This means you can only see the directory because it's in the path of a directory or file where you do have rights. If you get this message, just press ESCAPE to make it go away, and move to a directory where you have rights to see files (File Scan right).

Selective File Listings

In addition to listing a directory's files with FILER, you can do selective file listings with NDIR. Selective file listings let you list only the files that match the criteria you specify.

Listing Files Based on Last-Accessed Date

1. Type

   NDIR

   The interactive menu will appear, with the cursor on "Filename." Press ENTER, and the cursor will move to "None." Use the right arrow key to highlight "Access" and press ENTER.

   You will see a line that looks like this:

   chronologically < > = < > =

   The cursor will be on the "<" symbol. If you want to see files accessed before a certain date, this is what you want. If you want to see files accessed after a certain date, choose the ">" symbol.

2. Press ENTER.

3. Specify the month, day, and year. For example, to specify January 3, 1990, you would type

   01 03 90

   You needn't press ENTER after each specification.

4. Press END, and your list will be displayed.

Listing Files Based on Last Update

1. Type

      NDIR

   The interactive menu will appear, with the cursor on "Filename." Press ENTER, and the cursor will move to "None." Use the right arrow key to highlight "Update" and press ENTER.

   You will see a line that looks like this:

      chronologically < > = < > =

   The cursor will be on the "<" symbol. If you want to see files accessed before a certain date, this is what you want. If you want to see files accessed after a certain date, choose the ">" symbol.

2. Press ENTER.

3. Specify the month, day, and year. For example, to specify January 3, 1990, you would type

      01 03 90

   You needn't press ENTER after each specification.

4. Press END, and your list will be displayed.

Listing Your Own Files in a Shared Directory

To list your own files in a shared directory, use the "Owner" option in the interactive menu.

1. Type

   NDIR

   The interactive menu will appear, with the cursor on "Filename." Press ENTER, and the cursor will move to "None."

2. Use the right arrow key to highlight "Owner."

3. Press ENTER.

   You will see a line that looks like this:

   alphabetically < > = < > =

   The cursor will be on the "=" symbol. In this context, the symbol means "is," which is what you want, so press ENTER.

4. Type your username and press ENTER.

5. Press END, and your list will be displayed.

Sorting File Lists by Size

1. Type

     NDIR

The interactive menu will appear, with the cursor on "Filename."

2. Use the right arrow key to highlight "Size" and press ENTER.

3. Now press END, and your list will be displayed.

Sorting File Listings by Date Last-Accessed

1. Type

    NDIR

    The interactive menu will appear, with the cursor on "Filename."

2. Use the right arrow key to highlight "Access" and press ENTER.

3. Now press END, and your list will be displayed.

Sorting File Listings by Last Update

1. Type

   NDIR

   The interactive menu will appear, with the cursor on "Filename."

2. Use the right arrow key to highlight "Update" and press ENTER.

3. Now press END, and your list will be displayed.

Copying Files

To copy files, complete these steps.

1. Access FILER.

2. Go to the directory you want to copy your files from (the "source" directory).

   NOTE: If you are copying your files from floppy diskettes or a local hard drive, you'll have to use COPY or NCOPY. FILER cannot copy FROM a local drive, although it can copy TO a local drive.

3. Choose "Directory Contents."

4. Choose the file(s) you want to copy. To choose more than one, use the F5 key to mark each.

5. Choose "Copy File" (if you want to leave a copy of the file at the source) or "Move File" (if you don't want a copy left at the source).

6. Specify the destination (target) directory. If you know it, just type it in. If you don't, press INSERT and choose directories until you've specified it. Then press ESCAPE and ENTER.

7. Specify the file's name. If you want it to have the same name, accept the default. If you want to rename it, type a new name. Then press ENTER.

Deleting and Renaming Files

From time to time, you will want to "clean up" and reorganize your files. That's when you'll want to know how to delete and rename them. Here's how.

1. Access FILER.

2. Go to the directory which contains the files you want to delete or rename.

3. Choose "Directory Contents."

4. To DELETE files,

   Highlight the file you want to delete. (To choose more than one, use the F5 key to mark each.)

   Press the DELETE key.

   Answer "Yes" when you're asked if you want to delete the file(s).

5. To RENAME a file,

   Highlight the file.

   Press the MODIFY (F3) key.

   Type the file's new name.

   Press ENTER.

Backing Up and Restoring Files

You may want to substitute a short explanation of your backup policy for the generic paragraph below. And, if you have diskless workstations or do not require users to back up their files, delete this section entirely.

Even though we back up network files regularly, you should still back up your personal files as a precaution. You don't need to back up all your files every day; just back up the ones you've changed that day.

For most users, the simplest thing to do will be to back up to a floppy diskette as explained here.

To back up your files, just copy them to a floppy diskette by completing these steps:

1. Access FILER.

2. Choose "Directory Contents."

3. Highlight the file(s) you want to copy. To choose more than one, mark each with the Mark (F5) key.

4. Press ENTER.

5. Choose "Copy File."

6. Specify the drive for the floppy diskette you want to copy the file(s) to (A: or B:).

7. Press ENTER, and the file(s) will be copied.

Printing Files

Generally, I don't recommend that you teach users how to print their files with NetWare. This is why.

- For most users, it will be much easier to simply print using applications. If you set up network printing properly and test it thoroughly, printing from applications should be transparent to users.

- NetWare printing is complex, and users need to understand it fairly well to be comfortable with the NetWare printing utilities. Generally, it makes more sense to set up custom menus for users to print with than to educate users about the many printing parameters.

However, if you do wish to teach your users how to print with NetWare menu utilities, you can include this short explanation of NetWare printing and the PCONSOLE command in their manuals.

Printing on a network is a little more involved than printing with a regular personal computer. Instead of going directly from your personal computer to the printer, print data must follow a somewhat more complex path. This path was set up when the network was installed, so you shouldn't have to worry about it. But briefly, it is as follows.

First, the print data ("print job" in NetWare terms) goes to a network print queue, which is located on the file server's hard disk. Like the personal computer's buffer or spool area, the print queue is a waiting area for print jobs that pile up faster than they can be printed. However, a network print queue stores jobs from many different users. Which queue your print jobs go to depends on how network printing has been set up, or which queue you specify when you print the job.

> You may wish to tell them which print queue(s) their print jobs will go to, and why, here.

A process called a print server takes print jobs out of the queue and sends them to the printer. As with print queues, print servers are established when network printing is set up. Which queues a print server services, and which printers it sends print jobs to, depends on how network printing was set up.

> You may wish to tell them which printer(s) their print jobs will go to, and why, here.

Luckily, you don't really need to know all this information to print a file. If the file was created in a network application or text editor, just print it from there. If the file was created in a non-network application or text editor, you can print it with NPRINT. The following section summarizes how.

Type...	...to
NPRINT *filename*	Print a file created in a non-network application or text editor.
NPRINT *filename* NOTI	Be notified when a job has finished printing.
NPRINT *filename* C=*n*	Print a certain number of copies (replace *n* with the desired number)

Working with Directories

Most of the time, when you clean up and reorganize, you'll be working with files. But sometimes you will also want to work with the directory structure itself.

The following section summarizes how to create, rename, and delete directories, as well as how to copy directory structures.

Create a Directory

1. Access FILER.

2. Move to the directory beneath which you would like to create the subdirectory, if you're not already there.

3. Choose "Directory Contents."

4. Press INSERT.

5. Type the new directory's name and press ENTER.

Rename a Directory

1. Access FILER.

2. Move to the directory's parent directory.

3. Choose "Directory Contents."

4. Highlight the directory you want to rename.

5. Press the MODIFY (F3) key.

6. Type the directory's new name.

Delete a Directory

1. Access FILER.

2. Move to the directory's parent directory.

3. Choose "Directory Contents."

4. Highlight the directory you want to delete.

5. Press the DELETE key.

6. Answer "Yes" when asked if you want to delete the directory.

Ideas for Creating Your Own Directory Structure

The directory structure for the file server organizes files for everyone who works on the file server. In the areas where you keep your own personal files, you may wish to create your own small directory structures to organize your files. In fact, if you will have more than a few files, this is a good idea: you shouldn't dump your electronic files on a computer without organizing them any more than you'd dump your paper files on a desk or in a drawer.

As you plan your directory structure, consider these questions.

1. What will I organize my files based on?

   Consider what files you have to manage, and what kind of structure would help you organize them well. It may be useful to think of how you would organize ordinary paper files efficiently, and use that as a guideline for planning your directory structure.

2. Will other people will need to access my files?

   If so, it may make sense to put files that need to be accessed by the same people in the same directories.

3. What should I name my directories?

   Give your directories meaningful, descriptive names.

4. How many levels deep should I make my directory structure?

   Generally, it's best not to make the directory structure more than three or four levels deep.

If you start getting a lot of files in a directory, consider subdividing the directory and reorganizing your files.

Once you have decided how you want to organize your personal directories, use the FILER command to create them according to your plan. Complete these steps.

1. Access FILER.

2. Move to the directory beneath which you would like to create the subdirectory, if you're not already there.

3. Choose "Directory Contents."

4. Press INSERT.

5. Type the new directory's name and press ENTER.

Setting Up Drive Mappings

> Most users probably won't need to set up drive mappings, and even fewer will need to set up search drive mappings. The main reason to set up a search drive mapping is if the user will use personal applications on the network.
>
> In addition, drive and search drive mappings consume directory entries. If you're concerned about excessive drive mappings consuming directory entries, you may not want to teach your users how to set up mappings.
>
> Also, if you didn't include the previous sections explaining drive and search drive mappings, you won't want to include this section.

You probably won't need to set up drive mappings to your newly-created subdirectories unless your subdirectory structure is quite deep and complex. In most cases, it will be easier to use your existing drive mappings to get to the general area, then move up and down the directory structure. But if you do want to set up drive mappings, here's how to do it.

1. Access SESSION.

2. Choose "Drive Mappings."

3. Press INSERT.

4. Press ENTER.

5. Choose subdirectories until you have specified the directory you wish to map the drive to.

6. Press ESCAPE.

7. Press ENTER.

Saving Mappings in Login Scripts

The next part of this section tells how to save mappings in personal login scripts. If you teach users how to save drive mappings in their login scripts, caution them not to inadvertently override the mappings contained in the system-wide login script.

Drive mappings set up at the command line last only until you log out. Most of the time, you will want your drive mappings to be more permanent than that. To have your drive mappings set up every time you log in, you must save them in your login script. Here's how to do so.

1. Access the SYSCON utility.

2. Choose "User Information."

3. Choose your name.

4. Choose Login Script.

   You'll see your login script. It may have many or few commands, depending on how your supervisor has set it up. Be very careful when you're working in the login script. Make sure you understand the intent of each line before you make any changes.

5. To set the drive mapping, type

   MAP *n:=*directory path*

6. Exit SYSCON, saving your changes.

Setting Security

Setting security is a fairly advanced topic that most users won't really be concerned with. If you have set up the high-level directory structure properly, users should not have to worry about other users accessing their personal files. Some users may create files in their personal directories that they share with other users; these are probably the·only users who might be concerned with setting security.

Remember, unless a user has the Supervisory or Access Control right in a directory, he or she can not set security anyway. So skip this section for all users who do not have these rights anywhere.

Also, if you include this section, make sure you included the full explanation of security previously, since users need to understand inherited rights masks and trustee rights before they set security.

In the directories where you have the Supervisory or Access Control right, you can set security if you wish. Unless you create directories or files which you need to share with other users, you probably won't need to do this, however.

If you do need to assign security, follow these steps.

1. Decide which users need which rights in your directories.

   You may want to sketch the directory tree and write in the names of users who need access to certain directories, along with what rights they should be given. Remember, once you have granted a trustee right in a directory, the right trickles down the tree. So you may not need to actually make trustee assignments in every single directory where you want the user to have security privileges.

You may also want to refer to the following rights table as you decide what rights to grant.

Letter	Right	Lets you ...
S	Supervisory	Exercise all rights for directory or file
R	Read	Directory level: Open a directory's files and read them or copy them to other directories
		File level: Open a file and read it or copy it to another directory
W	Write	Directory level: Change contents of files in directory
		File level: Change contents of file
C	Create	Directory level: Create files and subdirectories
		File level: Salvage deleted files; create and write a file
E	Erase	Directory level: Delete empty directories
		File level: Delete the file
M	Modify	Directory level: Change directory attributes; rename subdirectories and files
		File level: Change the file's attributes; rename the file
F	File Scan	Directory level: See files and subdirectories
		File level: See the file
A	Access Control	Assign security for directory or file

2. Decide if you want to limit the rights that users can inherit into any given directory.

   Sometimes, you want to be sure that a certain right cannot be inherited into a given directory. For example, you may want to make sure that no one can inherit the Erase right into a given directory. When this is the case, you should set the directory's inherited rights mask so the directory masks the right.

   Remember, an inherited rights mask blocks users' inherited rights only for the directory to which the mask is assigned.

   If you sketched the directory tree, write in the inherited rights masks on your sketch.

3. Check to be sure that the trustee assignments and inherited rights masks that you have planned give users the rights you want them to have in your directories.

4. Make trustee assignments.

   For each directory where you wish to make a trustee assignment,

   a.. Access FILER.

   b. Go to the directory where you wish to make the trustee assignment(s) (if you're not already there).

   c. Choose "Current Directory Information."

   d. Choose the "(see list)" field next to the "Trustees" label (it's at the bottom of the screen).

    e. The current trustees will be shown. Most likely, there won't be any.

    f. Press INSERT.

    g. Choose the user(s) and/or group(s) you wish to make trustees of the directory. To choose more than one, mark each with the F5 key.

5.   Now that the trustees are added, change their rights if necessary.

    a. Choose the trustee(s) whose rights you wish to change. To choose more than one, mark each with the F5 key.

    b. The current trustee rights will be shown. To remove a right, highlight it and press DELETE. To remove more than one, mark each right you wish to remove with the F5 key and press DELETE.

    c. Choose "Yes."

Complete the above steps for every trustee assignment you wish to make. Remember that trustee rights trickle down through the directory structure, so you needn't make a trustee assignment in every directory where you want a user to have rights.

6.   Change directory rights masks, if necessary, by completing these steps.

    a. Access FILER.

    b. Choose "Current Directory Information."

    c. Choose the bracketed field next to "Inherited Rights Mask" at the bottom of the screen.

d.   To delete a right from the mask,

Highlight the right(s).

Press DELETE.

Answer "Yes."

Set Directory Attributes

The last step in setting security is to set directory attributes if necessary.

1. Access FILER.

2. Go to the directory whose attributes you wish to set.

3. Choose "Current Directory Information."

4. Choose the "see list" field next to the "Directory Attributes" label. (It's in the middle of the screen.) The directory's current attributes (also called "flags") will be shown.

5. Press INSERT.

6. Choose the attribute(s) you wish to add. To choose more than one, mark each with the F5 key.

7. Press ESCAPE, and the directory will be flagged with the attributes you chose.

Conclusion

> The following generic conclusion is based on the unmodified Manual Maker text for this chapter. Modify it based on how you modified the chapter.

In this chapter, you learned about

- Directory structures, directory paths, and directory names

- Moving around the directory tree with FILER and drive mappings

- NetWare security and how it controls what you can do on the network

- Working with files, including listing, copying, deleting, renaming, backing up and restoring, printing, and purging

- Working with directories, including listing, creating, copying, deleting, and renaming

- Setting up your own drive mappings

- Establishing security in your personal areas of the directory structure

Command Line Utilities Reference

The text for this boilerplate chapter is found in
CLUS.WP (WordPerfect version)
CLUS.ASC (ASCII version)

This chapter features simple explanations of the NetWare command line utilities. Only utilities of use to non-administrative users are included.

For the sake of simplicity, these explanations don't include every available task and option; rather, the most common tasks and options are included. But remember, you can always add to or delete from the explanations given here, based on your needs.

Deciding Which Utilities to Include

You can include whatever utilities you want in your users' manuals, of course. (You can even add non-NetWare utilities ued on your network if you like.) But if you don't know exactly which utilities you want to include, the following comments may help you decide. You can also use the comments contained throughout the Manual Maker.

Delete these utilities if...	Utility	Page
...the user will never need to work with more than one file server.	ATTACH	214
	SLIST	263
	WHOAMI	269
...the user doesn't know anything at all about security.	ALLOW	211
	FLAG	226
	FLAGDIR	228
If the user does know about security, include utilities based on the user's knowledge:	GRANT	230
	REMOVE	252
	REVOKE	256
	RIGHTS	259
	TLIST	265
Cross off these utilities if the user will never assign security.	ALLOW	211
	GRANT	230
	REMOVE	252
	REVOKE	256
	TLIST	265
Cross off these utilities if the user doesn't know about security attributes.	FLAG	226
	FLAGDIR	228
If the user knows anything about security at all, INCLUDE this utility.	RIGHTS	259

Delete these utilities if...	Utility	Page
...the user will always use an AUTOEXEC.BAT file to log in.	LOGIN	234
...you do not want the user to purge files.	PURGE	249
...the user will never need to check the system time.	SYSTIME	264
...the user will never need to see space usage information.	CHKDIR	220
	CHKVOL	221
...users won't use the NetWare SEND command to send eachother messages.	CASTOFF/ CASTON	217
	SEND	261
	USERLIST	268
...the user doesn't know anything about network printing.	CAPTURE	215
...the user doesn't know about drive mappings.	MAP	236
...the user doesn't know about directory structures.	CD	219
	LISTDIR	233
	RENDIR	255
...users will never change the passwords of their own accord (because you force password changes).	SETPASS	262
...the user will never delete or rename files.	DEL	223
	REN	254
...the user will never copy files.	NCOPY	241

Making a Master List of Users' Rights

In many cases, a user must have certain rights in order to perform a task. These cases are noted throughout this chapter. Sample text is also provided if you want to tell users in which directories they can perform certain tasks.

Before you begin modifying this chapter, you may want to print up a master list of users' rights throughout the directory tree. This will come in handy as you go through the chapter.

Here are the steps.

1. Log in as the user.

2. List the user's effective right throughout the tree by typing

   WHOAMI /R

3. Print the resulting list by completing these steps.

   A. Type

        Capture TI=10

   B. Press the SHIFT and PRTSCR keys simultaneously.

Keep the resulting list handy as you work through this chapter.

CHAPTER 6

Command Line Utilities Reference

This chapter explains the Command Line utilities in reference form. Here are the utilities that are covered, in alphabetical order.

ALLOW

Include if user

- Understands NetWare security thoroughly (including security rights, effective rights, trustee rights, and inherited rights masks)

- Will need to restrict access to any directories (probably only in personal directories if at all; File Scan and Supervisory or Access Control right required)

Few users use this command.

View, set, or modify the inherited rights mask of a directory or file.

Since users can not work with inherited rights masks unless they have the appropriate rights, you may wish to list the directories and/or files where the user has these rights. You can use the following sample text to do so if you wish.

On our network, you can work with the inherited rights masks of these directories:

<List the directories where the user has the File Scan and Supervisory or Access Control rights here; refer to your master list of the user's rights throughout the directory tree if desired (see page 207 of the unmodified Manual Maker).>

Task	Type
View current directory's inherited rights mask	ALLOW .
View the inherited rights mask of a file in your current directory	ALLOW *filename*
Change your current directory's inherited rights mask	ALLOW *rightslist* (replace *rightslist* with the abbreviations for the desired rights, with a space between each letter)
Change the inherited rights mask of a file in your current directory	ALLOW *filename rightslist* (replace *rightslist* with the abbreviations for the desired rights, with a space between each letter)

A brief explanation of the NetWare security rights is contained in the following table. You may wish to include it here for users' convenience.

Here's a brief explanation of the NetWare security rights.

Letter	Right	Lets you ...
S	Supervisory	Exercise all rights for directory or file
R	Read	Directory level: Open a directory's files and read them or copy them to other directories
		File level: Open a file and read it or copy it to another directory
W	Write	Directory level: Change contents of files in directory
		File level: Change contents of file
C	Create	Directory level: Create files and subdirectories
		File level: Salvage deleted files; create and write a file
E	Erase	Directory level: Delete empty directories
		File level: Delete the file
M	Modify	Directory level: Change directory attributes; rename subdirectories and files
		File level: Change the file's attributes; rename the file
F	File Scan	Directory level: See files and subdirectories
		File level: See the file
A	Access Control	Assign security for directory or file

ATTACH

Include if

• Network has more than one file server

• User has an account on more than one of those servers and accesses those accounts manually (not via a batch file or login script)

If the user accesses an additional server more often than not, you may want to include the appropriate ATTACH command in his or her login script. This way, the user attaches to the additional server automatically upon logging in. All the user has to do is enter a password, if one is required.

Access additional servers once you've logged in to your primary server.

Task	Type
Attach to another file server	ATTACH *fileserver/username*
	Then enter password if prompted.
	Example:
	ATTACH GADFLY/STEVE

CAPTURE

Include if user

- Prints documents not created in network applications

- Does such printing manually (not via menus, login scripts, or batch files)

Unless you have advanced, inquisitive users who often print outside applications, I recommend that you don't teach users about CAPTURE. Instead, include this command in their login scripts or in the system login script:

CAPTURE TI=10

This way, the local LPT port is captured when users log in, and they can print as usual, by pressing SHIFT + PRT SCR. Print jobs are automatically sent to the printer after 10 seconds (or the time you specify after the TImeout parameter— you may want to use a larger number if print jobs use soft fonts or lots of graphics).

Print files not created in a network application. The Create option also allows you to save print output to a network file.

Task	Type
Print from non-network application without exiting from it	CAPTURE TI=10
Print upon entering or exiting an application	CAPTURE AUTOENDCAP
Store print output in a file	CAPTURE CR=*filename*
Be told when your job has printed	CAPTURE TI=10 NOTIfy
Print more than one copy of a job	CAPTURE TI=10 C=*number*

CASTOFF/CASTON

Include if users

- Send messages with SEND or SESSION

- Want to block such messages from time to time (if many messages are sent across the network, and they don't want to be interrupted)

CASTOFF/CASTON were originally developed because when a message sent with SEND (or SESSION) is received, the message disables workstation processing until it is cleared with CTRL-ENTER. If a user is away from a station when a message is received, any processing being done at the station will be stopped until the user returns and clears the message. CASTOFF solves this potential problem by allowing a user disable message reception at the workstation; CASTON then allows the user to re-enable message reception.

You can teach your users about CASTOFF/CASTON if you want. Or, you can analyze when users might need to use CASTOFF (What tasks do they perform that involve lengthy processing which shouldn't be interrupted?). Then, set up a batch file to begin the task, and include CASTOFF in the batch file. If a user is certain that he or she doesn't want to be interrupted by network messages, include CASTOFF in his or her login script. Or, you can create a group (for example, "Hermits"), and include all such users in the group. Then, in the system login script, include this line:

IF MEMBER_OF_GROUP "HERMITS" THEN #CASTOFF

Block messages sent from all network stations; enable your workstation to receive messages again.

Task	Type
Block messages sent to you with SEND or SESSION	CASTOFF
Enable your workstation to receive messages again	CASTON

CD (DOS Command)

Include if user

- Knows about directory structures (all users except extreme novices should)

- Moves up and down the directory structure manually (not with drive mappings or menus)

Move up and down the directory structure.

Task	Type
Move up one directory level	CD ..
Move up two directory levels	CD ...
Move to the root directory	CD \
Move down one directory level	CD *subdirectory*
	Example: CD PERSONAL
Move down two directory levels	CD *subdir\subdir*
	Example:
	CD PERSONAL\LETTERS

CHKDIR (DOS Command)

Include if user

- Is concerned with managing space on file server

- Does troubleshooting that involves checking space usage information (such as checking to see why a file can't be saved)

See information about the space on a file server, volume, and directory.

Task   **Type**

See space usage statistics   CHKDIR
(current directory)

See space usage statistics   CHKDIR *path*
(not current directory)

Examples:

CHKDIR G:
CHKDIR LETTERS

CHKDIR returns information similar to this:

```
Directory Space Limitation Information For:
LATE\SYS:SYSTEM

Maximum              In Use           Available

56,352 K             9,084 K          47,268 K   VolumeSize
                     1,912 K          47,268 K   \SYSTEM
```

CHKVOL

Include if user

- Is concerned with managing space on file server

- Does troubleshooting that involves checking space usage information (such as checking to see why a file can't be saved)

See information about the space on a volume.

CHKVOL can only be used on network drives. If you try to check a local drive, there will be no response. Also, if you try to check a non-existent drive, there will be no response.

Task	What to Type
See space usage statistics for a volume	CHKVOL *volume*
See space usage statistics for all volumes on server	CHKVOL *

CHKVOL returns information similar to this:

```
Statistics for fixed volume LATE/SYS:


Total volume space:                    56,352  K Bytes
  Space used by files:                 9,088   K Bytes
  Space in use by deleted files:       120     K Bytes
  Space available from deleted files:120      K Bytes
  Space remaining on volume:           47,264  K Bytes
  Space available to SUPERVISOR:       47,264  K Bytes
```

DEL (DOS Command)

Include if user

- Deletes files with operating system (requires Erase right)

Erase a file.

Since users can not delete files unless they have the Erase right in a directory, you may wish to list the directories where the user has this right. You can use the following sample text to do so if you wish.

On our network, you can delete files in the following directories:

\<List the directories where the user has the Erase right here; refer to your master list of the user's rights throughout the directory tree if desired (see page 207 of the unmodified Manual Maker).\>

Task	Type
Erase a file (in your current directory)	DEL *filename*
Erase a file (not in your current directory)	DEL *path filename*

DIR (DOS Command)

> Include if user
>
> • Lists files and directories with operating system (most users should; requires File Scan right)

List a directory's files and subdirectories.

> Depending on your users' level of sophistication, you may also wish to include the following note:

You must have the appropriate security privileges to list a directory's files and subdirectories. If you don't, no files or subdirectories will be shown, although they may exist.

> Since users can not list files and subdirectories unless they have the File Scan right in a directory, you may also wish to list the directories where the user has this right. You can use the following sample text to do so if you wish.

On our network, you can list files and subdirectories of the following directories:

<List the directories where the user has the File Scan right here; refer to your master list of the user's rights throughout the directory tree if desired (see page 207 of the unmodified Manual Maker).>

Task	Type
List a directory's files and subdirectories, along with the dates they were last modified	DIR
List files and subdirectories (wide display)	DIR /W
List files and subdirectories, with a pause when the screen is full	DIR MORE

FLAG

Include if user

- Understands NetWare security attributes

- Needs to see file attributes (usually while troubleshooting to find out why a certain task, such as opening a file, cannot be performed)

- Sets attributes for files (requires File Scan and Modify rights)

Few users check attributes, and fewer still set them.

View or change file attributes.

Since users can not change file attributes unless they have the File Scan and Modify rights for a file, you may wish to list the directories and/or files where the user has these rights. You can use the following sample text to do so if you wish.

On our network, you can change the attributes of files in these directories:

<List the directories where the user has the File Scan and Modify rights here; refer to your master list of the user's rights throughout the directory tree if desired (see page 207 of the unmodified Manual Maker).>

Task	Type
View file attributes (current directory)	FLAG *filename*
Change file attributes (current directory)	FLAG *filename attributes* Example: FLAG INFOBASE S RW (flags the file INFOBASE Shareable, ReadWrite)
View file attributes (not current directory)	FLAG *path*
Change file attributes (not current directory)	FLAG *path attributes* Example: FLAG G:INFOBASE S RW (flags INFOBASE Shareable, ReadWrite)

File Attributes List

Here are the most common file attributes. Use the bolded letters to abbreviate.

Shareable—file can be opened by more than one user at a time

Read**O**nly—file can be read, but not changed

Read**W**rite—file can be changed

Hidden—hides file in DOS directory searches

Delete Inhibit—file cannot be deleted

Rename Inhibit—file cannot be renamed

FLAGDIR

Include if user

- Understands NetWare security attributes

- Needs to see directory attributes (usually while troubleshooting to find out why a certain task, such as opening a file, cannot be performed)

- Sets attributes for directories (requires File Scan and Modify rights)

Few users check attributes, and fewer still set them.

View or change directory attributes.

Since users can not change directory attributes unless they have the File Scan and Modify rights in the directory, you may wish to list the directories where the user has these rights. You can use the following sample text to do so if you wish.

On our network, you can change the attributes of the following directories:

<List the directories where the user has the File Scan and Modify rights here; refer to your master list of the user's rights throughout the directory tree if desired (see page 207 of the unmodified Manual Maker).>

Task	Type
View attributes (current directory)	FLAGDIR .
Change attributes (current directory)	FLAGDIR . *attributes*
View attributes (not current directory)	FLAGDIR *path*
Change attributes (not current directory)	FLAGDIR *path attributes*

Directory Attributes List

Here are the most common directory attributes. You can use the bolded letters to abbreviate.

Hidden—hides directory in DOS directory scans
Purge—files in directory will be purged upon deletion
Delete Inhibit—directory can't be erased
Rename Inhibit—directory can't be renamed

GRANT

Include if user

- Understands NetWare security thoroughly (including security rights, effective rights, trustee rights, and inherited rights masks)

- Needs to assign trustees in any directories (probably only in personal directories if at all; Supervisory or Access Control right required)

Few users use this command.

Grant users or groups trustee rights in a file or directory.

Since users can not grant trustee rights unless they have the Supervisory or Access Control right in a directory, you may wish to list the directories where the user has this right. Use the following sample text to do so if you wish.

On our network, you can grant trustee rights in the following directories:

<List the directories where the user has the Supervisory or Access Control right here; refer to your master list of the user's rights throughout the directory tree if desired (see page 207 of the unmodified Manual Maker).>

Task	Type
Grant rights (current directory)	GRANT *rights* TO *user*
	Example:
	GRANT R F TO VALERIE (Grants Read and File Scan rights to user VALERIE)
Grant rights (not current directory)	GRANT *rights* FOR *path* TO *user*
	Example:
	GRANT R F FOR BUSTED TO VALERIE

A brief explanation of the NetWare security rights is contained in the following table. You may wish to include it here for users' convenience.

Here's a brief explanation of the NetWare security rights.

Letter	Right	Lets you ...
S	Supervisory	Exercise all rights for directory or file
R	Read	Directory level: Open a directory's files and read them or copy them to other directories
		File level: Open a file and read it or copy it to another directory
W	Write	Directory level: Change contents of files in directory
		File level: Change contents of file
C	Create	Directory level: Create files and subdirectories
		File level: Salvage deleted files; create and write a file
E	Erase	Directory level: Delete empty directories
		File level: Delete the file
M	Modify	Directory level: Change directory attributes; rename subdirectories and files
		File level: Change the file's attributes; re-name the file
F	File Scan	Directory level: See files and subdirectories
		File level: See the file
A	Access Control	Assign security for directory or file

LISTDIR

Include if user

- Knows about directory structures (all users except extreme novices should)

- Lists a directory's subdirectories (File Scan right required to see directories marked System or Hidden)

Include the /R and /E options if user

- Understands NetWare security thoroughly (most users would look at their effective rights or the inherited rights mask when troubleshooting.)

View a directory's subdirectories, their inherited rights masks, and your effective rights in each.

Task	Type
View a directory's subdirectories	LISTDIR
View a directory's subdirectory tree	LISTDIR /S
View a directory's subdirectories and the inherited rights mask for each	LISTDIR /R
View a directory's subdirectories and your effective rights for each	LISTDIR /E

LOGIN

Include for all users unless you are certain that they will always log in automatically via AUTOEXEC.BAT files.

Log in to a file server.

Task	Type
Log in to a file server	LOGIN *fileserver/username*
	Then enter password if prompted.
	Example:
	LOGIN GADFLY/STEVE

LOGOUT

Include for all users unless they will log out from a menu or via some other method you've set up.

Log out from a file server.

You should always log out when you finish working on the network, or if you are going to be away from your workstation for awhile, so unauthorized users can't use your account.

Task   **Type**

Logout from a file server   LOGOUT

MAP

Include if user

- Understands directory structures

- Understands mappings

This explanation of MAP is divided into three sections that progress from basic to advanced.

- Approach #1 is for users who understand drive mappings and use them, but do not set up drive mappings.

- Approach #2 is for users who understand drive mappings and do set them up.

- Approach #3 is for users who understand search drive mappings.

Each section is self-contained; choose the one you want, and exclude the others.

MAP Approach #1:

For users who

- Understand and use drive mappings, but

- Won't set up their own mappings

View your drive mappings.

Task	Type
View your drive mappings	MAP

MAP Approach #2:

For users who

- Understand and use drive mappings

- Also set up their own drive mappings

View and set your drive mappings.

Task	Type
View your drive mappings	MAP
Set a drive mapping	MAP *driveletter*:=*path*

MAP Approach #3:

For users who

- Understand drive and search drive mappings

- Set up their own drive and search drive mappings

Task	Type
View your drive and search drive mappings	MAP
Set a drive mapping	MAP *driveletter*:=*path*
Set a search drive mapping	MAP S*number*:=*path*

Remember, drive and search drive mappings set up at the command line last only until you log out. If you want these mappings to be executed every time you log in, include the above commands in your login script (taking care not to override other drive and search drive mappings).

MD (DOS Command)

> Include if user
>
> • Understands directory structures
>
> • Creates directory structures (usually under home directory; Create right required)

Make a directory.

> Since users can not create a subdirectory beneath a directory unless they have the Create right in that directory, you may wish to list the directories where the user has these rights. You can use the following sample text to do so if you wish.

On our network, you can create directories in the following locations:

<List the directories where the user has the Create right here; refer to your master list of the user's rights throughout the directory tree if desired (see page 207 of the unmodified Manual Maker).>

Task	Type
Make a directory	MD *directory*
	Example:
	MD LETTERS

NCOPY

Include if user

- Copies files with operating system (requires Read and File Scan rights in the source directory, and the Create right in the target directory)

Copy files between network directories and/or local drives or hard disks.

Since users can not copy files unless they have the appropriate rights, you may wish to list the directories where the user has these rights. You can use the following sample text to do so.

On our network, you can copy files to and from these directories.

Dirs. You Can Copy Files From

<List the directories here—
User must have Read and
File Scan rights in them>

Dirs. You Can Copy Files To

<List the directories here—
User must have the Create right
in them>

Task	Type
Copy file to current directory	NCOPY *path filename*
	Example:
	NCOPY G:REPORTS
Copy file from current directory filename path to another directory	NCOPY
	Example:
	NCOPY REPORT G:
Copy file and rename at the same time	NCOPY *filename newname*
	Example:
	NCOPY REPORTS RESEARCH
Copy multiple related files	Use wildcards
	Example:
	NCOPY *.BAT

NDIR

Include if user

- Lists directories and files with operating system (most users should)

- Needs to see more information than DIR provides

- Needs to sort and restrict file listings beyond the abilities DIR provides

NDIR is a powerful command that lets you sort and restrict file and directory listings based on all sorts of criteria. Unfortunately, NDIR can also be very complex. You may prefer to have novice users use DIR, since DIR returns less information.

In addition, unless NDIR is used quite often, it can be difficult to remember the syntax. Fortunately, there are a couple of ways around this. You can use NDIR's interactive menu option (explained in Chapter 7 of the unmodified Manual Maker). Or, you can create a custom menu whose options call the appropriate variation of the NDIR command, then have users use that menu.

This explanation of NDIR does NOT explain every NDIR option available; for simplicity's sake, I included only those options I thought would be useful to the average nonadministrative user. You can add to, or delete from, my material if you want to, of course.

List files and subdirectories and see information about them. You can also sort and/or restrict the results of lookups based on the criteria you specify.

> Depending on your users' level of sophistication, you may also wish to include the following note:

You must have the appropriate security privileges to list a directory's files and subdirectories. If you don't, no files or subdirectories will be shown, although they may exist.

> Since users can not list files and subdirectories unless they have the File Scan right in a directory, you may wish to list the directories where the user has this right. You can use the following sample text to do so if you wish.

On our network, you can list files and subdirectories of the following directories:

<List the directories where the user has the File Scan right here; refer to your master list of the user's rights throughout the directory tree if desired (see page 207 of the unmodified Manual Maker).>

Task	Type
List a directory's files and subdirectories, and information about them	NDIR .
Sort lists by size, smallest to largest	NDIR SORT SIZE
Sort lists by last update, earliest to latest	NDIR SORT UPDATE
Sort lists by when they were last accessed, earliest to latest	NDIR SORT ACCESS
See only files updated before or after a certain date	NDIR UPDATE BEFore|AFTer *mm-dd-yy* Example: NDIR UPDATE AFT 01-25-90 (lists only files created after January 25, 1990)

See only files accessed before or
after a certain date

ACCESS BEFore|AFTer *mm-dd-yy*

Example:

NDIR ACCESS AFT 02-15-90 FO (lists
only files accessed before February 15,
1990)

See only files created by a
certain person

NDIR OWNER=*username*

Example:

NDIR OWNER=CHRIS
(lists only files created by user Chris)

See files only (no subdirectories)

NDIR FO
(FO = Files Only)

See directories only (no files)

NDIR DO
(DO = Directories Only)

See subdirectory tree under
directory

NDIR SUB
(SUB = SUBdirectory)

NPRINT

Include if user

- Prints existing, pre-formatted files from outside of network applications

NPRINT offers many options that allow users to specify exactly how they want a job to be printed. However, unless a user understands NetWare printing very well and uses NPRINT quite often, these options can be difficult to remember and use. For most users, it makes sense to create a menu that calls the relevant NPRINT commands. Then have the user use the menu instead of trying to train the user about all the available options.

The following task table explains only a few NPRINT options. If you include the Form option, make sure your users know which forms are available.

Print existing, previously-formatted files from outside of an application.

Task	Type
Print an existing, previously-formatted file from outside of an application	NPRINT *filename*
Print more than one copy of the file	NPRINT *filename* C=*number*
Print the job on a certain form	NPRINT *filename* FORM=*formname*
	Available forms include:
	<list and describe forms here>

PURGE

Include if user

- Needs to purge files (most users won't)

PURGE is a potentially dangerous command for users to know about. Users can not purge files they can not delete, so they can not do any more damage than their security allows. On the other hand, they may purge a file or files that they will want to recover later.

It's up to you if you want to teach your users about PURGE, of course. If you prefer to purge the system periodically yourself, it's probably best not to tell users about this command.

Permanently erase deleted files.

Since users can not purge files unless they have the Erase right in a directory, you may wish to list the directories where the user has this right. You can use the following sample text to do so if you wish.

On our network, you can purge files in the following directories:

<List the directories where the user has the Erase right here; refer to your master list of the user's rights throughout the directory tree if desired (see page 207 of the unmodified Manual Maker).>

Task	Type
Purge an erased file	PURGE *filename*
Purge all erased files (current directory)	PURGE
Purge all erased files throughout directory's subdirectory tree	PURGE /A

RD (Remove Directory—DOS Command)

Include if user

- Understands directory structures

- Deletes directories (usually under home directory, while reorganizing files; Erase right required)

Erase a directory.

Since users can not erase a directory unless they have the Erase right in its parent directory, you may wish to list the directories where the user has this right. You can use the following sample text to do so if you wish.

On our network, you can delete subdirectories beneath these directories:

<List the directories where the user has the Erase right here>

Task	Steps
Erase directory	1. Go to the directory's parent directory.
	2. Type
	RD *directory*

REMOVE

Include if user

- Understands NetWare security thoroughly (including security rights, effective rights, trustee rights, and inherited rights masks)

- Needs to remove a trustee from directories (probably only in personal directories if at all; Supervisory or Access Control right required)

Few users use this command.

Delete a user or group from the trustee list of a directory.

Users and groups can also be deleted from the trustee list of a file, since security can be assigned at the file level in NetWare 386. However, few users should be involved with security at this level, so that option isn't covered here.

Since users can not remove trustees unless they have the Supervisory or Access Control right in a directory, you may wish to list the directories where the user has this right. You can use the following sample text to do so if you wish.

On our network, you can remove trustees from the following directories:

<List the directories where the user has the Supervisory or Access Control right here; refer to your master list of the user's rights throughout the directory tree if desired (see page 207 of the unmodified Manual Maker).>

Task	Type
Remove user from current directory	REMOVE *user*
Remove user from all of directory's subdirectories	REMOVE *user subdirectory*

REN (DOS command)

Include if user

• Renames files with operating system (probably only in personal directories, while reorganizing; Modify right required)

Rename a file.

Since users can not rename files unless they have the Modify right in a directory, you may wish to list the directories where the user has this right. You can use the following sample text to do so if you wish.

On our network, you can rename files in these directories:

<List the directories where the user has the Modify right here>

Task	Type
Rename file (in current directory)	REN *filename newname*
Rename file (not in current directory)	REN *path filename newname*

RENDIR

> Include if user
>
> - Renames directories with operating system (probably only beneath personal directories, while reorganizing; Modify right required. Also note that the Rename Inhibit attribute can't be set for the directory.)

Rename a directory.

> Since users can not rename a directory unless they have the Modify right in the directory's parent directory, you may wish to list the directories where the user has this right. You can use the following sample text to do so if you wish.

On our network, you can rename subdirectories of these directories:

<List the directories where the user has the Modify right here>

Task	Steps
Rename directory.	1. Go to parent directory.
	2. Type
	RENDIR *directory newname*

REVOKE

Include if user

- Understands NetWare security thoroughly (including security rights, effective rights, trustee rights, and inherited rights masks)

- Needs to assign trustee rights in any directories (probably only in personal directories if at all; Supervisory or Access Control right required)

Few users use this command.

Revoke some of a user's trustee rights in a directory.

Since a user can not revoke other users' trustee rights unless the user has the Supervisory or Access Control right in a directory, you may wish to list the directories where the user has one or both of these rights. You can use the following sample text to do so if you wish.

On our network, you can revoke rights in the following directories:

<List the directories where the user has the Supervisory or Access Control right here; refer to your master list of the user's rights throughout the directory tree if desired (see page 207 of the unmodified Manual Maker).>

Task	Steps
Revoke some of a user's rights in a directory	1. Go to the directory
	2. Type
	REVOKE *rightslist* FROM *username*
	Example:
	REVOKE M FROM JENNIFER
	(revokes user Jennifer's Modify right in current directory)

> A brief explanation of the NetWare security rights is contained in the following table. You may wish to include it here for users' convenience.

Here's a brief explanation of the NetWare Security rights.

Letter	Right	Lets you ...
S	Supervisory	Exercise all rights for directory or file
R	Read	Directory level: Open a directory's files and read them or copy them to other directories
		File level: Open a file and read it or copy it to another directory
W	Write	Directory level: Change contents of files in directory
		File level: Change contents of file
C	Create	Directory level: Create files and subdirectories
		File level: Salvage deleted files; create and write a file
E	Erase	Directory level: Delete empty directories
		File level: Delete the file
M	Modify	Directory level: Change directory attributes; rename subdirectories and files
		File level: Change the file's attributes; re-name the file
F	File Scan	Directory level: See files and subdirectories
		File level: See the file
A	Access Control	Assign security for directory or file directories

RIGHTS

Include if user

- Knows about NetWare security

- Checks effective rights (usually when troubleshooting to find out why a certain task, such as saving a file, cannot be performed. Only users who understand the NetWare security rights would ever do this.)

See your effective rights in a directory.

Users could also see their effective rights for individual files, since security can be assigned at the file level in NetWare 386. However, few users should be involved with security at this level, so that option isn't covered here.

Task	Type
See your effective rights (current directory)	RIGHTS
See your effective rights (not current directory)	RIGHTS *path*
	Example:
	RIGHTS H: (shows your effective rights for the directory which is mapped to drive H:)

A brief explanation of the NetWare security rights is contained in the following table. You may wish to include it here for users' convenience.

Here's a brief explanation of the NetWare security rights.

Letter	Right	Lets you ...
S	Supervisory	Exercise all rights for directory or file
R	Read	Directory level: Open a directory's files and read them or copy them to other directories
		File level: Open a file and read it or copy it to another directory
W	Write	Directory level: Change contents of files in directory
		File level: Change contents of file
C	Create	Directory level: Create files and subdirectories
		File level: Salvage dclctcd files; create and write a file
E	Erase	Directory level: Delete empty directories
		File level: Delete the file
M	Modify	Directory level: Change directory attributes; rename subdirectories and files
		File level: Change the file's attributes; rename the file
F	File Scan	Directory level: See files and subdirectories
		File level: See the file
A	Access Control	Assign security for directory or file

SEND

Include if user
• Sends short messages to other users at the command line

Send a short message to another network user or group.

Task	Type
Send a message to a network user or group	SEND *"message" name*
	Example:
	To send the message "Want to go to lunch?" to user Kelley, you would type
	SEND "WANT TO GO TO LUNCH?" TO KELLEY
Send a message to more than one user or group	SEND *"message" name, name network*
	Example:
	To send the message to users Kelley and Ev, you would type
	SEND "WANT TO GO TO LUNCH?" TO KELLEY, EV

SETPASS

Include unless

- You are one of very few installations that don't require passwords

- You force periodic password changes and are certain that users will only change their passwords then

Change your password.

Task	Steps
Change your password	1. Type
	SETPASS
	2. Type your old password.
	3. Type your new password.
	4. Retype your new password.

SLIST

Include if

- Your network has more than one file server

- User will ever need to list the file servers that are currently active on the network (most users would do this if they have accounts on more than one server, or wish to send a message to a user on another server)

List the other file servers on your network that your file server can currently communicate with.

Task	Type
See the servers which your file server can communicate with	SLIST

SYSTIME

Include if user

- Needs to see the system time

- Needs to synchronize workstation time with file server time (if user does time-dependent tasks that require precise synchronization between file server and workstation)

Few users need to use this command.

If it is important for workstation time to remain precisely synchronized with the file server time on your network, I recommend that you include SYSTIME in a login script or batch file. That way, the workstation and file server time will be synchronized when the user logs in.

See the file server's date and time, and synchronize your workstation's date and time with it.

Task	Type
See your file server's current time	SYSTIME

TLIST

Include if user

- Understands NetWare security thoroughly (including security rights, effective rights, trustee rights, and inherited rights masks)

- Has the Supervisory or Access Control right in any directories (necessary to list trustees)

- Needs to list trustees (the main reason to list trustees in day-to-day use is for troubleshooting. Some users might like to see who else has rights in a directory out of curiousity—mainly in their personal directories—but even this is unlikely)

Few users use this command.

List the trustees of a directory and their rights.

Since users can not list the trustees of a directory unless they have the Supervisory or Access Control right in the directory, you may wish to list the directories where the user has one or both of these rights. You can use the following sample text to do so if you wish.

On our network, you can list trustees of the following directories:

<List the directories where the user has the Supervisory or Access Control right here; refer to your master list of the user's rights throughout the directory tree if desired (see page 207 of the unmodified Manual Maker).>

Task	Type
List trustees (current directory)	TLIST
List trustees (not current directory)	TLIST *path*

> A brief explanation of the NetWare security rights is contained in the following table. You may wish to include it here for users' convenience.

Here's a brief explanation of the NetWare security rights.

Letter	Right	Lets you ...
S	Supervisory	Exercise all rights for directory or file
R	Read	Directory level: Open a directory's files and read them or copy them to other directories
		File level: Open a file and read it or copy it to another directory
W	Write	Directory level: Change contents of files in directory
		File level: Change contents of file
C	Create	Directory level: Create files and subdirectories
		File level: Salvage deleted files; create and write a file
E	Erase	Directory level: Delete empty directories
		File level: Delete the file
M	Modify	Directory level: Change directory attributes; rename subdirectories and files
		File level: Change the file's attributes; re-name the file
F	File Scan	Directory level: See files and subdirectories
		File level: See the file
A	Access Control	Assign security for directory or file

USERLIST

> Include if users
>
> - Lists other users logged into the file server (for curiosity, or to send messages with the SEND command)

List the users who are currently logged in to a server.

Task	Type
List users currently logged in to server	USERLIST

WHOAMI

> Include if
>
> - There is more than one file server on the network
>
> - User periodically logs in to several servers at a time
>
> Include /R, /S, and /G options if
>
> - The user understands network security

View information about yourself as a network user.

Task	Type
See your username and login date/time	WHOAMI
See your effective rights	WHOAMI /R
See your security equivalences	WHOAMI /S
See your group membership	WHOAMI /G

Menu Utilities Reference

The text forthis boilerplate chapter is found in
MENU.WP (WordPerfect version)
MENU.ASC (ASCII version)

This chapter features simple explanations of the NetWare menu utilities. Only utilities used by non-administrative users are included, and only tasks used by non-administrative users are documented. Tasks are documented by utility, in sequential order, based on how the utility is constructed.

Deciding Which Tasks to Include

You can include whatever utilities you like in your user manuals, of course. (You can even add non-NetWare utilities used on your network if you like.) But if you don't know exactly which utilities you want to include, the following comments may help you decide. You can also use the comments contained throughout the Manual Maker.

1. Delete these tasks if the user never needs to work with more than one file server.

   Change Your Current Server, 335 and 344

2. Delete these tasks if the user doesn't know anything at all about security.

   View Directory Owner, Creation Date/Time, Effective Rights, Maximum
      Rights Mask, 279
   View/Change Directory Attributes, 282
   Change Inherited Rights Mask, 285
   View/Change Directory Trustees, 288
   List Groups, 345
   See Group's Full Name, 346
   See Members of Group, 349
   See Trustee Assignments (Groups), 350
   See Trustee Assignments (Your Own), 370
   See the Groups You Belong To, 361
   See Security Equivalences, 364
   See Trustee Directory Assignments, 368

3. Delete this task if you have not established accoutning on your server, or if the user doesn't know anythng about accounting.

   See Your Account Balance, 354

4. Delete this task if users never set up passwords of their own accord (because you have set up forced password changes.)

Change Your Password, 359

5. Delete these tasks if you have not established the related restrictions, or if you prefer simply to tell the user what the restrictions are.

See Your Account Restrictions, 355
See Station Restrictions, 365
See Time Restrictions, 366
See Volume Restrictions, 371

6. Delete these tasks if the user doen't know anything about NetWare printing.

List Print Jobs, 320
Print a File, 322
Print Job Parameters, 324

7. Delete these tasks if the user doen't know about drive or search drive mappings.

View/Set Drive Mappings, 336
View/Set Search Drive Mappings, 339
Select Default Drive, 341

8. Delete these tasks if the user does not use NetWare to send messages.

>   Send a Message to a Group, 338
>   Send a Message to a User, 342

9. Delete this task if the user doesn't know about volumes.

>   See Volume Information, 313

10. Most users won't need to know how to do these tasks. Check the Comments to see if you want to include them.

>   Set Filer Options, 312
>   See Your Full Name, 360

Making a Master List of User' Rights

In many cases, a user must have certain rights to perform a task. These cases are noted throughout this chapter. Sample text is also provided if you want to tell users what directories they can do certain tasks in.

Before you begin modifying this chapter, you may want to print a master list of user' rights throughout the directory tree. Here are the steps.

1. Log in as the user.

2. Clear the screen by typing,

    CLS

3. List the user's effective rights throughout the structure by typing,

    WHOAMI /R

4. Print the resulting list by completing these steps.

    A. Type

    CAPTURE TI=10

    B. Press the SHIFT and PRTSCR keys simultaneously.

Keep the printed list handy as you work through this chapter.

CHAPTER 7

Menu Utilities Reference

This chapter explains the Menu utilities in reference form. Here are the tasks that are covered.

FILER Tasks

```
┌────────────────────────────────────────────┐
│            Available Topics                 │
├────────────────────────────────────────────┤
│  Current Directory Information              │
│  Directory Contents                         │
│  Select Current Directory                   │
│  Set Filer Options                          │
│  Volume Information                         │
└────────────────────────────────────────────┘
```

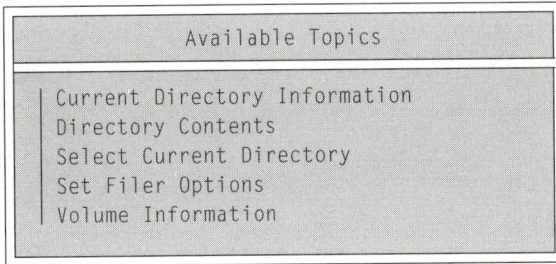

View Directory Owner, Creation Date/Time, Attributes, Effective Rights, Inherited Rights Mask (FILER)

Include if user

- Knows about NetWare security

- Needs to see directory attributes (usually while troubleshooting to find out why a certain task, such as opening a file, cannot be performed)

- Checks effective rights (usually when troubleshooting to find out why a certain task, such as saving a file, cannot be performed. Only users who understand the NetWare security rights would ever do this)

- Needs to see a directory's inherited rights mask (usually when troubleshooting to figure out how effective rights were determined. Only users with a very thorough understanding of NetWare security—including security rights, effective rights, trustee rights, and inherited rights masks—would ever do this)

Unless users have a thorough understanding of NetWare security, much of the information in this screen will be extraneous—and possibly confusing. For this reason, you might want to have them use the RIGHTS command to see their effective rights, and the FLAG or FLAGDIR command to see file and directory attributes.

A directory's owner is the person who created the directory. Your effective rights are those you can actually exercise in the directory, and the directory's inherited rights mask shows which inherited rights the directory will prevent from being exercised.

Action	**Display**
1. Access FILER.	FILER "Available Topics" menu
2. Choose "Current Directory Information."	Directory Information" screen

Example follows:

```
┌─────────────────────────────────────────┐
│    Directory Information for SCREENS     │
├─────────────────────────────────────────┤
│ Owner: SUPERVISOR                        │
│ Creation Date: October 9, 1990           │
│ Creation Time: 12:55 pm                  │
│ Directory Attributes: (see list)         │
│ Current Effective Rights: [SRWCEMFA]     │
│ Inherited Rights Mask: [SRWCEMFA]        │
│                                          │
│ Trustees: (see list)                     │
└─────────────────────────────────────────┘
```

A brief explanation of the NetWare security rights is contained in the following table. You may wish to include it here for users' convenience.

Here's a brief explanation of the NetWare security rights.

Letter	Right	Lets you ...
S	Supervisory	Exercise all rights for directory or file
R	Read	Directory level: Open a directory's files and read them or copy them to other directories File level: Open a file and read it or copy it to another directory
W	Write	Directory level: Change contents of files in directory File level: Change contents of file
C	Create	Directory level: Create files and subdirectories File level: Salvage deleted files; create and write a file
E	Erase	Directory level: Delete empty directories File level: Delete the file
M	Modify	Directory level: Change directory attributes; rename subdirectories and files File level: Change the file's attributes; rename the file
F	File Scan	Directory level: See files and subdirectories File level: See the file
A	Access Control	Assign security for directory or file

Change Directory Attributes (FILER)

Include if user

• Understands NetWare security attributes

• Sets attributes for directories (probably only in personal directories; Modify right required)

Very few users change directory attributes.

Since users can not change directory attributes unless they have the Modify right in a directory, you may wish to list the directories where the user has this right. You can use the following sample text to do so if you wish.

Directory attributes, along with rights, determine what can be done with the files in a directory.

On our network, you can change the attributes of the following directories:

<List the directories where the user has the Modify or Supervisory right; refer to your master list of the user's rights throughout the directory tree if desired (see page 276 of the unmodified Manual Maker).>

Action	Display
1. Access FILER.	FILER "Available Topics" menu
2. Choose "Current Directory Information."	"Directory Info." display
3. Choose "(see list)" field next to "Directory Attributes."	"Current Flags" list
4. To ADD an attribute,	"Other Search Attributes"
a. Press Insert.	
b. Choose the attribute.	"Current Flags" (with attribute shown)
5. To DELETE an attribute,	
a. Highlight attribute.	"Delete Search Attribute"
b. Press DELETE.	"Current Flags" (with attribute deleted)
c. Answer "Yes."	

Directory Attributes List

Here's a quick explanation of directory attributes.

Delete **I**nhibit—prevents the directory from being deleted
Hidden—hides directory
Purge—purges directory upon deletion
Rename **I**nhibit—prevents the directory from being renamed

Change Inherited Rights Mask (FILER)

Include if user

- Understands NetWare security thoroughly (including security rights, effective rights, trustee rights, and inherited rights masks)

- Assigns security (probably only in personal directories, if at all; Supervisory or Access Control right required)

Few users change inherited rights masks.

Since users can not change the inherited rights mask unless they have the Supervisory or Access Control right in a directory, you may wish to list the directories where the user has this right. You can use the following sample text to do so if you wish.

A directory's inherited rights mask filters the rights users inherit into a directory.

On our network, you can change the inherited rights mask for the following directories:

<List the directories where the user has the Supervisory or Access Control right here; refer to your master list of the user's rights throughout the directory tree if desired (see page 276 of the unmodified Manual Maker).>

Action	**Display**
1. Access FILER.	FILER "Available Topics" menu
2. Choose "Current Directory information."	"Directory Information" screen
3. Choose the bracketed field next to "Inherited Rights Mask" at the bottom of the screen.	"Inherited Rights" menu
4. To add a right to the mask,	
a. Press Insert.	"Other Rights" list
b. Choose the right(s).	"Inherited Rights" menu with rights added
5. To delete a right from the mask,	
a. Highlight the right(s).	
b. Press DELETE.	"Revoke Right" prompt
c. Answer "Yes."	"Inherited Rights" menu with right(s) revoked

A brief explanation of the NetWare security rights is contained in the following table. You may wish to include it here for users' convenience.

Here's a brief explanation of the NetWare security rights.

Letter	Right	Lets you ...
S	Supervisory	Exercise all rights for directory or file
R	Read	Directory level: Open a directory's files and read them or copy them to other directories File level: Open a file and read it or copy it to another directory
W	Write	Directory level: Change contents of files in directory File level: Change contents of file
C	Create	Directory level: Create files and subdirectories File level: Salvage deleted files; create and write a file
E	Erase	Directory level: Delete empty directories File level: Delete the file
M	Modify	Directory level: Change directory attributes; re name subdirectories and files File level: Change the file's attributes; rename the file
F	File Scan	Directory level: See files and subdirectories File level: See the file
A	Access Control	Assign security for directory or file

View/Change Directory Trustees (FILER)

Include if user

- Understands NetWare security thoroughly (including security rights, effective rights, trustee rights, and inherited rights masks)

- Has the Supervisory or Access Control right in any directories (necessary to list or assign trustees)

- Needs to list trustees (the main reason to list trustees in day-to-day use is for troubleshooting. Some users might like to see who else has rights in a directory out of curiousity—mainly in their personal directories—but even this is unlikely)

- Needs to assign trustees in any directories (probably only in personal directories if at all)

Few users use this command.

Since users can not view or assign trustees unless they have the Supervisory or Access Control right in a directory, you may wish to list the directories where the user has one or both of these rights. You can use the following sample text to do so if you wish.

A directory's trustees are those users who have been given direct security privileges for the directory.

On our network, you can change the trustees of the following directories:
<List the directories where the user has the Supervisory or Access Control right here; refer to your master list of the user's rights throughout the directory tree if desired (see page 276 of the unmodified Manual Maker).>

Action	**Display**
1. Access FILER	FILER "Available Topics" menu
2. Choose "Current Directory Information."	"Directory Information" screen
3. Choose the "(see list)" field next to the "Trustees" label at the bottom of the screen.	List of trustees and their rights
4. To add a trustee,	
a. Press Insert.	"Others" list
b. Choose the user(s) you wish to make trustees.	List of trustees with new trustees added
5. To delete a trustee,	
a. Highlight trustee(s).	
b. Press DELETE.	"Delete Trustee From Directory" prompt
c. Choose "Yes."	List of trustees with trustee(s) deleted

6. To change a trustee's rights,

    a. Highlight the trustee.

    b. Then, to add a right, press   "Other Rights" menu
       Insert and choose the right(s).   Rights added

    c. To delete a right, highlight   "Revoke Right?" prompt
       the right, press DELETE,
       and answer "Yes."

View a Directory's Files and Subdirectories (FILER)

Include if user

- Lists files and directories with operating system (most users should; requires File Scan right)

You must have the appropriate security privileges to list a directory's files and subdirectories. If you don't, no files or subdirectories will be shown, although they may exist.

You may wish to list the directories whose contents the user can see. You can use the following sample text to do so if you wish.

On our network, you can view the files and subdirectories of these directories:

\<List directories where user has the File Scan right\>

Action	Display
1. Access FILER.	FILER "Available Topics" menu
2. Choose "Directory Contents."	Directory's files and subdirectories

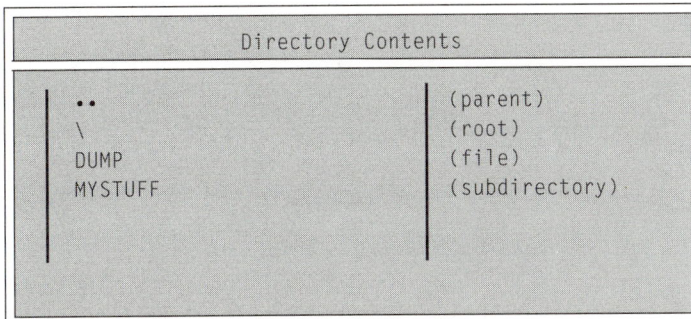

```
                    Directory Contents

   ..                                    (parent)
   \                                     (root)
   DUMP                                  (file)
   MYSTUFF                               (subdirectory)
```

Delete a File (FILER)

Include if user

- Deletes files with operating system (requires File Scan and
  Erase rights; file must not be flagged Delete Inhibit)

Since users can not delete files unless they have the File Scan and Erase rights in a directory, you may wish to list the directories where the user has these rights. You can use the following sample text to do so if you wish.

On our network, you can delete files in the following directories:

<List the directories where the user has the File Scan and Erase rights here; refer to your master list of the user's rights throughout the directory tree if desired (see page 276 of the unmodified Manual Maker).>

Action	Display
1. Access FILER.	FILER "Available Topics" menu
2. Choose "Directory Contents."	Directory's files and subdirectories
3. Highlight the file you want to delete.	File highlighted
4. Press DELETE.	"Delete file?" prompt
5. Answer "Yes."	File deleted

Rename a File (FILER)

> Include if user
>
> - Renames files with operating system (probably only beneath home directory, while reorganizing; File Scan and Modify rights required, and file must not be flagged Rename Inhibit)

Rename a file.

> Since users can not rename files unless they have the File Scan and Modify rights in a directory, you may wish to list the directories where the user has this right. You can use the following sample text to do so if you wish.

On our network, you can rename files in these directories:

<List the directories where the user has the File Scan and Modify rights here>

Action	Display
1. Access FILER.	FILER "Available Topics" menu
2. Choose "Directory Contents."	Directory's files and subdirectories
3. Highlight the file you want to delete.	File highlighted
4. Press MODIFY (F3).	"Edit File Name" prompt
5. Delete the file's old name.	
6. Type the file's new name.	

Copy a File (FILER)

> Include if user
>
> - Copies files with operating system (requires the File Scan and Read rights in the source directory, and the Create right in the target directory)

Copy files between network directories and/or local drives or hard disks.

> Since users can not copy files unless they have the appropriate rights, you may wish to list the directories where the user has these rights. You can use the following sample text to do so if you wish.

On our network, you can copy files to and from these directories:

Dirs. You Can Copy Files From

<List the directories here—
User must have the File Scan
and Read rights in them>

Dirs. You Can Copy Files To

<List the directories here—
User must have the Create right
in them>

Action	Display
1. Access FILER.	FILER "Available Topics" menu
2. Choose "Directory Contents."	Directory's files and subdirectories
3. Highlight the file(s) you want to copy.	File(s) highlighted
4. Press ENTER.	"File Options" Menu
5. Choose "Copy Files."	"Destination Directory" entry box
6. Specify the directory you want to copy the files to.	
7. Press ENTER.	Files will be copied

Move a File (FILER)

> Include if user
>
> - Moves files with operating system (requires the Read and Erase rights in the source directory, and the Create right in the target directory)

Move files between network directories and/or local drives or hard disks. (When a file is copied, a copy of the file remains at the source directory; when a file is moved, a copy does NOT remain at the source directory.)

> Since users can not move files unless they have the appropriate rights, you may wish to list the directories where the user has these rights. You can use the following sample text to do so if you wish.

On our network, you can move files to and from these directories.

Dirs. You Can Move Files From

<List the directories here—
User must have the Erase and
Read rights in them>

Dirs. You Can Move Files To

<List the directories here—
User must have the Create right
in them>

Action	**Display**
1. Access FILER.	FILER "Available Topics" menu
2. Choose "Directory Contents."	Directory's files and subdirectories
3. Highlight the file(s) you want to move.	File(s) highlighted
4. Press ENTER.	"File Options" Menu
5. Choose "Move File."	"Destination Directory" entry box
6. Specify the directory you want to move the files to.	"New Name" entry box
7. If you wish to rename the file, delete the old name and type the new. Otherwise, continue with the next step.	
8. Press ENTER.	File(s) will be moved

View a File's Contents (FILER)

Include if user

- Wants to view a file's contents without retrieving it (usually to jog his or her memory during directory searches)

Since users can not view a file's contents unless they have the File Scan and Read rights for the file, you may wish to list the directories and/or directories where the user has these rights. You can use the following sample text to do so if you wish.

On our network, you can view the contents of files in these directories:

<List directories where user has the File Scan and Read rights>

Action	Display
1. Access FILER.	FILER "Available Topics" menu
2. Choose "Directory Contents."	Directory's files and subdirectories
3. Highlight the file(s) whose contents you want to see.	File(s) highlighted
4. Press ENTER.	"File Options" Menu
5. Choose "View File."	File's contents shown

View a File's Information (FILER)

Most of the information in the top half of the "File Information" screen is related to security; most of the information in the bottom half of the screen is related to file usage (date last accessed, archived, modified, etc.).

The majority of users would be interested in the file usage information; however, only users who understand security quite thoroughly would be interested in the security information.

If users only need to see the file usage information, I recommend that you delete this task and have them work with NDIR instead.

Since users can not view file information unless they have the File Scan right for the file, you may wish to list the directories where the user has this right. You can use the following sample text to do so if you wish.

On our network, you can view information for files in the following directories:

<List the directories where the user has the File Scan right here; refer to your master list of the user's rights throughout the directory tree if desired (see page 276 of the unmodified Manual Maker).>

Action	Display
1. Access FILER.	FILER "Available Topics" menu
2. Choose "Directory Contents."	Directory's files and subdirectories
3. Highlight the file whose information you want to see.	File highlighted
4. Press ENTER.	"File Options" Menu
5. Choose "View/Set File Information."	File information shown (explanations follow)

File Attributes List

Ro	Read Only	File can be opened and read, but not changed
Rw	Read Write	File can be changed
S	Shareable	File can be opened by more than one user at a time
H	Hidden	File is hidden in DOS directory searches unless user has File Scan rights
A	Archive	File has not been archived since last modified
Sy	System	Reserved for system files
T	Transactional	Protects files from data corruption with NetWare's sophisticated Transaction Tracking system
P	Purge	File will be purged upon deletion
RA	Read Audit	An audit trail of who has read the file will be kept
WA	Write Audit	An audit trail of when the file has been changed will be kept
C	Copy Inhibit	File cannot be copied
D	Delete Inhibit	File cannot be deleted
R	Rename Inhibit	File cannot be renamed

Create a Directory (FILER)

Include if user

- Understands directory structures

- Creates directory structures (usually under home directory; Create right required)

Since users can not create subdirectories beneath a directory unless they have the Create right in that directory, you may wish to list the directories where the user has this right. You can use the following sample text to do so if you wish.

On our network, you can create directories beneath these directories:

<List the directories where the user has the Create right here; refer to your master list of the user's rights throughout the directory tree if desired (see page 276 of the unmodified Manual Maker).>

Action	**Display**
1. Access FILER.	FILER "Available Topics" menu
2. Choose "Directory Contents."	Directory's files and subdirectories
3. Press INSERT.	"New Subdirectory Name" entry box
4. Type the subdirectory's name.	
5. Press ENTER.	"Directory Contents" with new subdirectory listed

Delete a Directory (FILER)

Include if user

- Understands directory structures

- Deletes directories (usually under home directory, while reorganizing files; Erase right required)

Erase a directory.

Since users can not erase a directory unless they have the Erase right in its parent directory, you may wish to list the directories where the user has this right. You can use the following sample text to do so if you wish.

On our network, you can delete subdirectories beneath these directories:

<List the directories where the user has the Erase right here>

Action	Display
1. Access FILER.	FILER "Available Topics" menu
2. Choose "Directory Contents."	Directory's files and subdirectories
3. Highlight the directory you wish to delete.	
4. Press DELETE.	"Delete Subdirectory Options"
5. Choose "Delete Entire Subdirectory Structure" or "Delete Subdirectory's Files Only," depending on which you want to do.	Prompt asking you to confirm your choice
6. Choose "Yes."	The action you chose will be performed

Rename a Directory (FILER)

Include if user

- Renames directories with operating system (probably only beneath home directory, while reorganizing; Modify right required, and Rename Inhibit attribute cannot be set)

Rename a directory.

Since users can not rename a directory unless they have the Modify right in the directory's parent directory, you may wish to list the directories where the user has this right. You can use the following sample text to do so if you wish.

On our network, you can rename subdirectories of these directories:

<List the directories where the user has the Modify right here>

Action	Display
1. Access FILER	FILER "Available Topics" menu
2. Choose "Directory Contents."	Directory's files and subdirectories
3. Highlight the subdirectory you wish to rename.	
4. Press MODIFY (F3).	"Edit Directory Name" entry box
5. Delete the old name.	
6. Type the directory's new name and press ENTER.	Directory appears in list with its new name

Copy All of a Subdirectory's Files (FILER)

Include if user

- Copies files with the operating system (requires File Scan and Read rights in the source directory, and the Create right in the target directory)

Since users can not copy files unless they have the appropriate rights, you may wish to list the directories where the user has these rights. You can use the following sample text to do so if you wish.

On our network, you can copy files to and from these directories.

Dirs. You Can Copy Files From

Dirs. You Can Copy Files To

<List the directories here—
User must have File Scan
and Read rights in them>

<List the directories here—
User must have the Create right
in them>

Action	**Display**
1. Access FILER.	FILER "Available Topics" menu
2. Choose "Directory Contents."	Directory's files and subdirectories
3. Choose the directory whose files you wish to copy.	"Subdirectory Options" menu
4. Choose "Copy Subdirectory's Files."	"Copy Subdirectory To" prompt

5. Specify the directory you wish to copy the files to.

    a. If you know it, type it in.

    b. If you don't, press Insert and choose levels until you have specified the desired directory.

6. Press ESCAPE.

7. Press ENTER.

Copy Subdirectory's Structure (FILER)

Include if user

- Understands directory structures

- Copies entire directory structures, along with their files (usually under home directory, while reorganizing; File Scan and Read required at source, Create and Write required at target)

A word of caution: When a subdirectory structure is copied, a copy of the entire structure remains at the source. So if disk space is limited, you may not want to teach users about this task. (Most of the time, users would want to move subdirectory structures, as opposed to copying them, anyway.)

Users must have File Scan and Read rights in the source directory, and for each subdirectory beneath it, to copy a subdirectory structure. They must also have the Create and Write rights in the target directory. Most users would only copy subdirectory structures between directories located beneath their personal directories.

Action	Display
1. Access FILER.	FILER "Available Topics" menu
2. Choose "Directory Contents."	Directory's files and subdirectories
3. Choose the directory whose structure you wish to copy.	"Subdirectory Options" menu
4. Choose "Copy Subdirectory's Structure."	"Copy Subdirectory To:" prompt

5. Specify the directory you wish to copy the subdirectory structure beneath.

    a. If you know the directory path, type it in.

    b. If you don't, press Insert and choose levels until you have specified the desired directory.

6. Press ESCAPE.

7. Press ENTER.

Make This Your Current Directory (FILER)

Include if

- You expect the user to work in FILER a lot (this task is mainly for convenience while working in FILER)

Action	Display
1. Access FILER.	FILER "Available Topics" menu
2. Choose "Directory Contents."	Directory's files and subdirectories
3. Choose the subdirectory which you wish to move to.	"Subdirectory Options" menu
4. Choose "Make This Your Current Directory.	Return to "Directory Contents" list; new directory path shown at top center of screen

Select Current Directory (FILER)

Include if

- The user understands directory structures

- The user moves around the directory structure while in FILER

Action	**Display**
1. Access FILER.	FILER "Available Topics" menu
2. Choose "Select Current Directory."	"Current Directory Path" prompt
3. Specify the directory you wish to make your current directory.	
a. If you know the directory path, type it in.	
b. If you don't, press Insert and choose levels until you have specified the desired directory.	
4. Press ESCAPE.	
5. Press ENTER.	

Set Filer Options (FILER)

Include if

• You expect the user to work in FILER a lot

• The user wants to specify how he or she will work while in FILER, or do selective directory and file lookups.

Few users do this task.

Action	**Display**
1. Access FILER.	FILER "Available Topics" menu
2. Choose "Set Filer Options."	"Filer Settings" (see below)

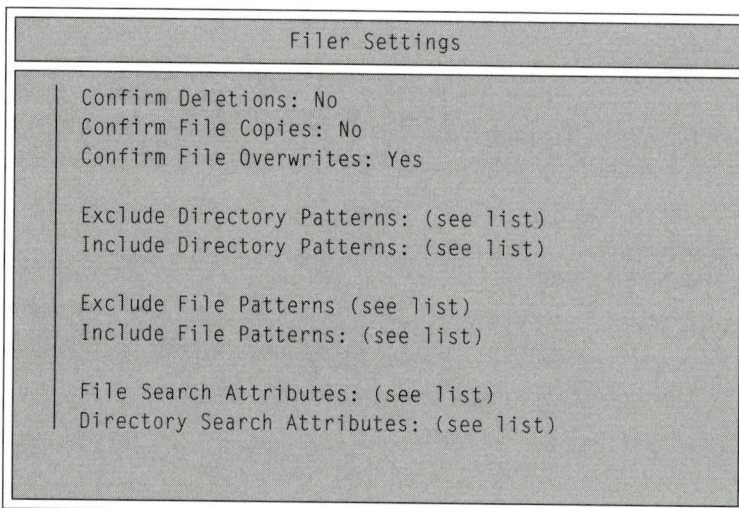

```
                    Filer Settings

     Confirm Deletions: No
     Confirm File Copies: No
     Confirm File Overwrites: Yes

     Exclude Directory Patterns: (see list)
     Include Directory Patterns: (see list)

     Exclude File Patterns (see list)
     Include File Patterns: (see list)

     File Search Attributes: (see list)
     Directory Search Attributes: (see list)
```

See Volume Information (FILER)

Include if the user ever needs to see

- How much directory space is left on a volume

- How many directory entries are available on a volume

(Only sophisticated users would understand this information. As supervisor, you should check this information often. However, nonadministrative users would probably check this information when troubleshooting to find out why a file cannot be saved, a directory cannot be created, or a directory cannot be mapped, since these operations involve directory space and directory entries.)

Action	**Display**
1. Access FILER.	FILER "Available Topics" menu
2. Choose "Volume Information."	Shown below.

Volume Information	
Server Name:	LATE
Volume Name:	SYS
Volume Type:	fixed
Total KBytes:	19,372
KBytes Available:	4,188
Maximum Directory Entries:	4,608
Directory Entries Available:	3,647

NDIR Tasks

```
  NDIR Options

    ┌─────────────────────────────────────────────────────────────┐
    │                                                             │
    │       To highlight options, use arrow keys                  │
    │       To select options, press Enter.                       │
    │       To start processing, press Spacebar.                  │
    │                                                             │
    │                                                             │
    └─────────────────────────────────────────────────────────────┘

    ->     SORT BY Filename Owner Size Update Create Access Archive
  RESTRCTIONS None Flags Owner Size Update Create Access Arc.

  PATH/FILE               Default Specify
  SCREEN FORMAT           Normal Dates Rights Macintosh
  DIRECTORIES             Current All
```

List a Directory's Subdirectories and Files (NDIR)

Include if user

- Lists directories and files with operating system (all users except extreme novices should)

- Needs to see more information than DIR provides

- Needs to sort and restrict file listings beyond the abilities DIR provides

NDIR isn't a menu utility per se, but it does have an interactive menu. That is why I have included NDIR in this chapter.

NDIR has many powerful options for sorting and/or restricting directory listings. Unfortunately, the very complexity which makes NDIR so powerful can also make it difficult to use at the command line. That is why the interactive menu has been provided. The menu is not like the standard menus used in SYSCON, FILER, etc., but it is easy to use. This section explains how to do so.

List files and subdirectories and see information about them. You can also sort and/or restrict the results of lookups based on the criteria you specify.

Depending on your users' level of sophistication, you may also wish to include the following note:

You must have the appropriate security privileges to list a directory's files and subdirectories. If you don't, no files or subdirectories will be shown, although they may exist.

> Since users can not list files and subdirectories unless they have the File Scan
> right in a directory, you may wish to list the directories where the user has this
> right. You can use the following sample text to do so if you wish.

On our network, you can list files and subdirectories of the following directories:

<List the directories where the user has the File Scan right here; refer to your
master list of the user's rights throughout the directory tree if desired (see page 276
of the unmodified Manual Maker).>

Here's how to use the NDIR menu.

1. Type

   NDIR

You'll then see a menu similar to the following:

```
 NDIR Options

    To highlight options, use arrow keys.
    To select options, press Enter.
    To bypass all options, press Spacebar.

    SORT BY              Filename Owner Size Update Create Access
                         Archive

    RESTRICTIONS         None Flags Owner Size Update Create Access
                         Archive

    PATH/FILE            Default  Specify

    SCREEN FORMAT        Normal Dates Rights Macintosh
```

When you enter this menu, you will see a blinking arrow next to the "SORT BY" option, and "Filename" will be highlighted.

2. Use the arrow keys to highlight the criterion (you can only choose one) you want to sort your lookup based on.

Filename	Alphabetical, based on filename
Owner	Owner of the file
Size	Size of the file
Update	Date last updated (earliest to latest)
Create	Date created (earliest to latest)
Access	Date last accessed (earliest to latest)
Archive	Date last archived (earliest to latest)

3. Press Enter.

You will see a blinking arrow by the "RESTRICTIONS" option. "None" will be highlighted. In addition, the "Normal" screen format option will be highlighted.

4. Use the arrow keys to highlight the criterion you want to use to restrict the results of your lookup.

None	No restrictions
Flags	See only files with given attributes (type them in the "Flag list" which is displayed when you choose this option)
Owner	See files listed by owners (choose an operator, then specify the first letters of the owner name)

Size	See only files of a given size (choose an operator, then specify a size)
Update	See only files updated before or after a certain date (choose an operator, then specify the date)
Create	See only files or directories created before or after a certain date (choose an operator, then specify the date)
Access	See only files accessed before or after a certain date (choose an operator, then specify the date)
Archive	See only files archived before or after a certain date (choose an operator, then specify the date)

5. Press ENTER.

   You will see a blinking arrow next to the "PATH/FILE" option, and the "Default" option will be highlighted.

6. Use this option to specify a directory path.

   A. To specify your current directory path, choose "Default."

   B. To specify another directory path, choose "Specify" and type the path.

7. Now choose the screen format:

Normal	Shows you the directory's subdirectories and files, their inherited rights masks, your effective rights for each, the owner of each, and the date and time created.

Dates   Shows you the directory's files, along with when they were created and the dates they were last modified, archived, or accessed. Shows the subdirectories, their inherited rights mask, your effective rights in each, the owner, and when created.

Rights   Shows you the directory's files, along with their attributes, inherited rights masks, your effective rights for each, and the owner of each. Shows the subdirectories, their inherited rights mask, your effective rights in each, the owner, and when created.

Macintosh   Shows you only directories and files created on a Macintosh machine.

8. Now specify whether you want the lookup to be for just your current directory (choose "Current"), or your current directory and its subdirectory tree (choose "All").

When you're done, the results of your lookup will be displayed.

The best way to learn how to use NDIR's interactive menu is to experiment. If you play with it for awhile, you'll soon realize what a powerful tool it is.

PCONSOLE Tasks

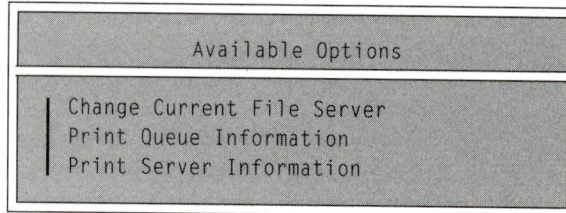

```
┌──────────────────────────────────────────┐
│            Available Options              │
├──────────────────────────────────────────┤
│  Change Current File Server               │
│  Print Queue Information                  │
│  Print Server Information                 │
└──────────────────────────────────────────┘
```

List Print Queues and Print Jobs (PCONSOLE)

Include if user

- Understands NetWare printing

- Has reason to look at all of the print jobs in a queue. (To look at print jobs this way, the user must know what queue[s] his or her print jobs go to. If you have more than one queue on your server, you may wish to tell users which queues their print jobs go to.)

Action	**Display**
1. Access PCONSOLE.	PCONSOLE "Available Topics" menu
2. Choose "Print Queue Information."	Print queues
3. Choose the print queue menu whose jobs you wish to view.	"Print Queue Information"
4. Choose "Current Print Job Entries."	Print jobs in queue

Seq	Banner Name	Description	Form	Status	Job
1	STEVE	BIKES.NEW	0	Ready	432
2	VAL	HUNKS	0	Ready	704

Print a file (PCONSOLE)

Include if

- User understands NetWare printing

- User prints files created in non-network applications

- You have not set up custom menus to be used for printing

This method of printing is somewhat cumbersome, and requires the user to have a fairly good knowledge of how NetWare printing works. Unless you have trained users thoroughly in how network printing works, I recommend that you don't teach them how to print a file this way. Instead, create an interactive menu or batch file that prompts the user for the file he or she wants to print, then prints it with the NPRINT command line utility.

Action	Display
1. Access PCONSOLE.	PCONSOLE "Available Options" menu.
2. Choose "Print Queue Information."	"Print Queues" list.
3. Choose the print queue you want to send the file to for printing.	"Print Queue Information" menu
4. Choose "Current Print Job Entries."	Current print job entries list (it may not have any entries in it)
5. Press INSERT.	"Select Directory to Print From" box

6. Specify the directory you want
   to print from. In most cases, this
   will be your current directory.

   Directory path will appear in box as
   you specify it

7. Press ENTER.

   "Available Files" list

8. Choose the file(s) you want
   to print. To choose more than one,
   highlight each and press MARK (F5).

   Highlighted file(s)

9. Press ENTER.

   "Print Job Configurations" list

10. Choose the desired print
    job configuration.

    "New Print Job to be Submitted" form

11. Change print job parameters
    if desired (see next page).

    Fields in form will change
    according to what you specify

12. Press ESCAPE.

    "Save Changes" menu

13. Choose "Yes."

    Print job will be inserted in queue

Print Job Parameters

Here's an explanation of the print job parameters shown in the "New Print Job to be Submitted" screen in PCONSOLE. Some of these parameters cannot be changed, and there are some that you won't want to change when you submit a print job initially. The parameters you might change are marked with an asterisk.

Print Job. This field is blank initially, since the print job hasn't actually been submitted yet.

Client. Your name.

Description. The file's name.

Status. This field is blank initially, since the print job hasn't actually been submitted yet.

User Hold. Should read "No" initially. (Can be changed to "Yes" to hold the print job later.)

Operator Hold. Should read "No" initially. (Can be changed to "Yes" to hold the print job later.)

Service Sequence. This field is blank initially, since the print job hasn't actually been submitted yet. Once the job is in the print queue, the number in this field shows the job's position in the queue.

Job Entry Date and Job Entry Time. These two fields show when the job was put in the print queue.

*Number of copies. How many copies to print.

*File Contents. Text or Byte Stream. "Text" tells the printer to translate tabs to spaces; "Byte Stream" tells the printer to send all characters directly to the printer without translation. In almost every case, use Byte Stream, especially if you are printing graphics, fonts, or any other file that has extensive printing commands.

*Tab size. The number of spaces the tabs should be converted to in your document, if you selected "Text."

*Suppress Form Feed. Change this field to "Yes" if your job prints with an extra blank page at the end.

*Notify when done. Specify "Yes" if you want to be told when your job has printed.

*Target server. The print server that services the job. (To list the available print servers, press ENTER. Then choose the server you want.)

*Form. The type of paper to print the job on. (To list the available forms, press ENTER. Then choose the form you want.)

*Print banner. Whether you want a print banner to print. A print banner is simply an extra sheet of paper that prints before the job and identifies the job name and who printed the job.

*Name. The username you want to print on the print banner. Identifies who printed the job.

*Banner name. The filename you want to print on the print banner. Identifies the job itself.

*Defer printing. Whether to print the job at a later time.

*Target date. If you have deferred printing, the date you want your job to print.

*Target time. If you have deferred printing, the time you want your job to print.

Delete a Print Job (PCONSOLE)

Include if user

- Understands NetWare printing

- Deletes print jobs with the operating system

Unless you are a print queue operator, you can only delete your own print jobs.

If the user is a print queue operator for any queues, you may wish to list those queues here.

You are a print queue operator for <list the queues here>. This means you can delete other users' print jobs in these queues.

Action	Display
1. Access PCONSOLE.	PCONSOLE "Available Options" menu
2. Choose "Print Queue Information."	"Print Queues" list
3. Choose the print queue which contains the job you want to delete.	"Print Queue Information" menu
4. Choose "Current Print Job Entries."	Current print job entries list
5. Highlight the job you want to delete and press DELETE.	"Delete Queue Entry" menu
6. Choose "Yes."	The print job is deleted

Change Order of Print Jobs (PCONSOLE)

Include if user

- Is a print queue operator.

If you include this task, you should also tell the user which queue(s) he or she is an operator for. Sample text follows.

You can only change the order of print jobs in a print queue if you are an operator for that print queue. You are a print queue operator for the following print queues:

<List print queues here>

Action	Display
1. Access PCONSOLE.	PCONSOLE "Available Options" menu
2. Choose "Print Queue Information"	"Print Queues" list
3. Choose the print queue which contains the job(s) whose order you wish to change.	"Print Queue Information" menu
4. Choose "Current Print Job Entries."	Current print job entries list
5. Choose the print job you wish to move.	"Print Queue Entry Information" screen
6. Highlight the "Server Sequence" parameter.	
7. Type the number of the position you wish to move the job to. (For example, to move a job to the top of the queue, you'd type "1".)	Parameter changes
8. Press ENTER.	
9. Press ESCAPE.	

Place a Hold on a Print Job (PCONSOLE)

Include if user

- Understands NetWare printing

You can only hold your own print jobs.

To hold a print job as explained here, a user must know which queue the job is in. For this reason, I suggest you tell users which print queue(s) their print jobs are sent to. Sample text follows.

When you print a file, it goes to one of these NetWare print queues:

<List the print queues here; explain what jobs go to what queues if necessary>

Action	**Display**
1. Access PCONSOLE.	PCONSOLE "Available Options" menu.
2. Choose "Print Queue Information."	"Print Queues" list
3. Choose the print queue which contains the job(s) whose order you wish to change.	"Print Queue Information" menu
4. Choose "Current Print Job Entries."	Current print job entries list
5. Choose the print job you wish to place a hold on.	"Print Queue Entry Information" screen
6. Highlight the "User Hold" field.	
7. Type "Y" for yes.	Status changes to "User Hold On Job"
8. Press ESCAPE.	List of print jobs (status of job you chose is now "Held")

View a Print Queue's Status (PCONSOLE)

Include this task if user

- Understands NetWare printing thoroughly

- Checks on whether or not a queue is active (probably when troubleshooting to figure out why a job isn't printing)

A print queue's status shows if the queue is active or inactive (servicing print jobs or not).

Action	Display
1. Access PCONSOLE.	"Available Options" menu
2. Choose "Print Queue Information."	"Print Queues" list
3. Choose the print queue whose status you wish to see.	"Print Queue Information" menu
4. Choose "Current Queue Status."	"Current Queue Status" screen

SALVAGE Tasks

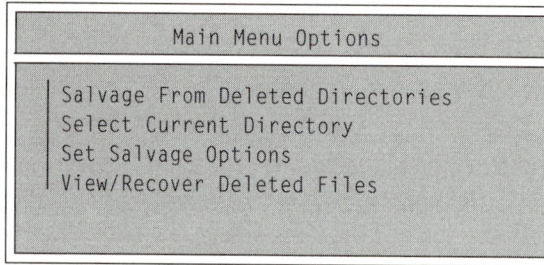

```
┌─────────────────────────────────────────────────┐
│              Main Menu Options                    │
├─────────────────────────────────────────────────┤
│  Salvage From Deleted Directories                 │
│  Select Current Directory                         │
│  Set Salvage Options                              │
│  View/Recover Deleted Files                       │
│                                                   │
└─────────────────────────────────────────────────┘
```

Salvaging Files

You may or may not want to teach users how to salvage files. It's a great feature and can save a lot of anxiety. But users should rarely have to use it, so you may just want to tell them that it's there and that if they need it, to contact their supervisor.

Sometimes you may delete or lose a file accidentally in spite of all your precautions. If this happens, all may not be lost. Often, you can salvage the file from the file server's hard disk using the SALVAGE menu utility.

SALVAGE works because there are two steps in deleting a file. The first is to mark it for deletion. (This is what you're actually doing when you delete a file with DELETE or ERASE.) Files marked for deletion actually stay on the hard disk until they are purged (permanently deleted), or the space they occupy is needed by other files. That's why you can often salvage an erased file by completing the following steps.

1. Access SALVAGE.

2. Go to the directory you want to salvage the files from, if it's not your current directory.

NOTE: Files must be salvaged from the directory they were in when they were deleted. If you deleted the directory as well as the files, your files can still be salvaged. However, the supervisor will have to help you. (If a file's directory is deleted, the file will be saved in special directory called DELETED.SAV. Since many users could have files in this directory, most users don't have rights to salvage from it.)

a. Choose "Select Current Directory."

b. Backspace to delete the parts of the path you don't want.

c. If you know the path, type it in. If you don't, press Insert and choose directories til you get to where you want.

d. Press ESCAPE.

e. Press ENTER.

Your current directory should be shown at the top of the screen, in the header.

3. If you want to sort the recoverable files based on certain criteria, specify those criteria.

a. Choose "Set Salvage Options."

b. Choose the menu option you want to sort the files based on.

4. Now you're ready to view the recoverable files.

a. Choose "View/Recover Deleted Files."

b. If you want to see only files which match a certain pattern, specify the pattern.

c. Press ENTER.

You'll see a list of all recoverable files, sorted as you specified.

d. Choose the file(s) you wish to recover.

To choose more than one, mark each with MARK (F5).

e. Answer "Yes."

The files will be recovered to their original directory.

SESSION Tasks

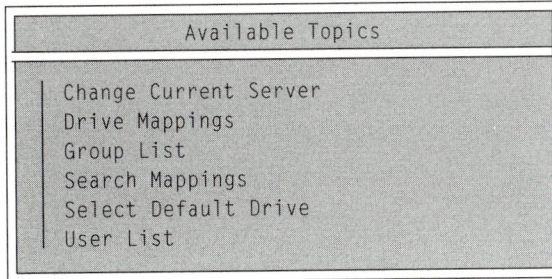

```
╔══════════════════════════════════════╗
║          Available Topics            ║
╠══════════════════════════════════════╣
║  │ Change Current Server             ║
║  │ Drive Mappings                    ║
║  │ Group List                        ║
║  │ Search Mappings                   ║
║  │ Select Default Drive              ║
║  │ User List                         ║
╚══════════════════════════════════════╝
```

Change Your Current Server (SESSION)

> Include if
>
> • Network has more than one file server
>
> • User has an account on more than one of those servers

Action	**Display**
1. Access SESSION.	"Available Topics" menu
2. Choose "Change Current Server."	File servers and usernames
3. Choose the file server you want to be your current server.	

View/Set Drive Mappings (SESSION)

Include if user understands

- Directory structures

- Drive mappings

Drive mappings are usually created with the MAP command and saved in login scripts so that they will be executed every time a user logs in. Drive mappings created in SESSION cannot be saved in login scripts, so drive mappings created here will last only the duration of a login session.

Action	Display
1. Access SESSION.	"Available Topics" menu
2. Choose "Drive Mappings."	"Current Drive Mappings" list

To add a drive mapping, continue with the following steps.

Action	Display
3. Press Insert.	"Drive:" prompt with next available drive letter displayed
4. Press ENTER.	"Select Directory" box
5. Press Insert and choose subdirectories until you have specified the directory you want to map the drive to.	
6. Press ESCAPE.	"Select Directory" box
7. Press ENTER.	"Current Drive Mappings" with drive mapping added

Send a Message to a Group (SESSION)

Include if user

- Sends short messages to other users at the command line

It's much faster to send messages with the SEND command than with SESSION. For this reason, I don't recommend SESSION unless you want your users to work exclusively with menu utilities.

Action	Display
1. Access SESSION.	"Available Topics" menu
2. Choose "Group List."	"Group List" menu
3. Choose the group you want to send a message to.	"Message:" entry box
4. Type the message and press ENTER.	The message will be sent to members of the group

View/Set Search Drive Mappings (SESSION)

Include if user understands

• Directory structures

• Search drive mappings

Search drive mappings are usually created with the MAP command and saved in login scripts so that they will be executed every time a user logs in. Search drive mappings created in SESSION cannot be saved in login scripts, so those created here will last only the duration of a login session.

Action	**Display**
1. Access SESSION.	"Available Topics" menu
2. Choose "Search Mappings."	"Current Search Mappings" list
To add a search drive mapping,	
3. Press Insert.	"Search Drive Number:" prompt with next available drive number displayed
4. Press ENTER.	"Select Directory" box

5. Press INSERT and choose
   subdirectories until you have specified
   the directory you want to map the search
   drive to.

6. Press ESCAPE.   "Select Directory" box

7. Press ENTER.   "Current Search Mappings" with new
                                              search drive mapping added.

Select Default Drive (SESSION)

> Include if user
>
> • Understands how drive mappings work
>
> • Uses drive mappings to move around in the directory structure
>
> I think this is easier to do at the command line. But if you have some real novice users, you might want to have them use SESSION.

Action	Display
1. Access SESSION.	"Available Topics" menu
2. Choose "Select Default Drive."	"Select Default Drive" list
3. Choose the drive you wish to make your current drive.	"Available Topics" menu

Send a Message to a User (SESSION)

> Include if user
>
> • Sends short messages to other users
>
> It's much faster to send messages with the SEND command than with SESSION. For this reason, I don't recommend SESSION unless you want your users to work exclusively with menu utilities.

Action	Display
1. Access SESSION.	"Available Topics" menu
2. Choose "User List."	"User List"
3. Choose the user(s) you want to send a message to.	"Message:" entry box
4. Type the message and press ENTER.	The message will be sent to the user(s).

SYSCON Tasks

```
┌─────────────────────────────────────────┐
│            Available Topic               │
├─────────────────────────────────────────┤
│  Accounting                              │
│  Change Current Server                   │
│  File Server Information                 │
│  Group Information                       │
│  Supervisor Options                      │
│  User Information                        │
│                                          │
│                                          │
└─────────────────────────────────────────┘
```

Only the SYSCON tasks that non-administrative users would be likely to perform are included here. These tasks are found under the "Change Current Server," "Group Information," and "User Information" options in the SYSCON main menu. Tasks included under the "Accounting," "File Server Information," and "Supervisor Options" menu options are not included in this chapter, because most non-administrative users wouldn't be concerned with the tasks listed under them.

Change Your Current Server (SYSCON)

Include if

• Network has more than one file server

• User has an account on more than one of those servers

Action

Display

1. Access SYSCON.

"Available Topics" menu

2. Choose "Change Current Server."

File servers and usernames

3. Choose the file server you want to log in to.

"Username" prompt

4. Type your username.

"Password" prompt

5. Type your password.

List Groups (SYSCON)

Include if user

- Understands NetWare security well enough to know that membership in a group gives him or her the same trustee rights as the group. (However, for this purpose, it's better to use the SYSCON "User Information" option to list the groups the user belongs to than to use this option to list all the groups on the server.)

- Will send messages to groups with the SEND command and wants to list the groups on a server. (However, for this purpose, it's better to just let them list the groups in SESSION, which they do as part of the process anyway.)

Generally, groups are a tool for supervisors to use in setting up the server efficiently. Most users won't have a lot to do with groups.

Action

1. Access SYSCON.

2. Choose "Group Information."

Display

"Available Topics" menu

"Group Names" list

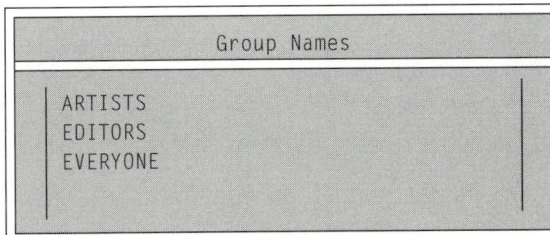

```
                 Group Names
 
   ARTISTS
   EDITORS
   EVERYONE
```

See Group's Full Name (SYSCON)

The ability to give a group a full name is meant mainly as a tool for supervisors (you can to look up a group's full name if you need to jog your memory). The average user will have little need to do this. Also, users can only see this information for a group if they are a member of it.

Action	Display
1. Access SYSCON.	"Available Topics" menu
2. Choose "Group Information."	"Group Names" list
3. Choose the appropriate group.	"Group Information" menu
4. Choose "Full Name."	Group's full name

See a Group's Managed Users and Groups (SYSCON)

Include if

- You have implemented the workgroup manager feature

- You have assigned a group to manage other users and groups

- The user belongs to this group

Managed users and groups are those that the group has been given administrative responsibility for.

Action	Display
1. Access SYSCON.	"Available Topics" menu
2. Choose "Group Information."	"Group Names" list
3. Choose the appropriate group.	"Group Information" menu
4. Choose "Managed Users and Groups."	"Managed Users and Groups" list

See a Group's Managers (SYSCON)

Include if

- You have implemented the workgroup manager feature

- You have assigned a manager or managers for the group

- The user belongs to this group

A group's manager is another group or user who has been given administrative responsibility for the group.

Action	Display
1. Access SYSCON.	"Available Topics" menu
2. Choose "Group Information."	"Group Names" list
3. Choose the appropriate group.	"Group Information" menu
4. Choose "Managers."	"Managers" list

See Members of Group (SYSCON)

Include if user

- Sends messages to groups, and may want to check who is in a group. (A user can only see the members of groups to which he or she belongs.)

- Understands security well enough to know that being a member of a group gives him or her the same trustee rights as the group has, and thus wants to see if he or she is in a group. (However, both the SYSCON "User Information" option and the WHOAMI /G command are better for this purpose.)

- May use groups to assign security

Action	Display
1. Access SYSCON.	"Available Topics" menu
2. Choose "Group Information."	Group menu
3. Choose the appropriate group.	"Group Information" menu
4. Choose "Member List."	Group members

See Trustee Directory Assignments (Groups) (SYSCON)

Include if user

- Has the Supervisory or Access Control right in any directories

- Knows about NetWare security (only users with a very thorough understanding of NetWare security—including security rights, effective rights,
trustee rights, and inherited rights masks—would ever want to list groups'
trustee assignments. Users would also have to understand that all members of a group have the same trustee rights as that group.)

Also note that users can only see this information for groups that they belong to.

These are the directories where the group has been given direct security privileges.

Action	Display
1. Access SYSCON.	"Available Topics" menu
2. Choose "Group Information."	Group menu
3. Choose the appropriate group.	"Group Information" menu
4. Choose "Trustee Directory Assignments."	"Trustee Directory Assignments" screen (see below)

```
┌─────────────────────────────────────────────────┐
│         Trustee Directory Assignments           │
├─────────────────────────────────────────────────┤
│   SYS:\                          [ RWCEMFA]      │
│   SYS:HOME                       [      F ]      │
│   SYS:HOME/CHRIS                 [ RWCEMFA]      │
│   SYS:MAIL/1A000004              [ RWCEMF ]      │
│   SYS:PLAY                       [ RWCEM A]      │
└─────────────────────────────────────────────────┘
```

A brief explanation of the NetWare security rights is contained in the following table. You may wish to include it here for users' convenience.

Here's a brief explanation of the NetWare security rights.

Letter	Right	Lets you ...
S	Supervisory	Exercise all rights for directory or file
R	Read	Directory level: Open a directory's files and read them or copy them to other directories File level: Open a file and read it or copy it to another directory
W	Write	Directory level: Change contents of files in directory File level: Change contents of file
C	Create	Directory level: Create files and subdirectories File level: Salvage deleted files; create and write a file
E	Erase	Directory level: Delete empty directories File level: Delete the file
M	Modify	Directory level: Change directory attributes; re name subdirectories and files File level: Change the file's attributes; rename the file
F	File Scan	Directory level: See files and subdirectories File level: See the file
A	Access Control	Assign security for directory or file

See Trustee File Assignments (Groups) (SYSCON)

Include if user

- Has been given the Supervisory or Access Control right in any directories

- Knows about NetWare security (only users with a very thorough under-standing of NetWare security—including security rights, effective rights, trustee rights, and inherited rights masks—would ever want to list groups' trustee assignments. Users would also have to understand that all members of a group have the same trustee rights as that group.)

Also note that users can only see this information for groups that they belong to.

These are the files where the group has been given direct security privileges.

Action	Display
1. Access SYSCON.	"Available Topics" menu
2. Choose "Group Information."	Group menu
3. Choose the appropriate group.	"Group Information" menu
4. Choose "Trustee File Assignments."	"Trustee File Assignments" screen

A brief explanation of the NetWare security rights is contained in the following table. You may wish to include it here for users' convenience.

Here's a brief explanation of the NetWare security rights.

Letter	Right	Lets you ...
S	Supervisory	Exercise all rights for directory or file
R	Read	Directory level: Open a directory's files and read them or copy them to other directories File level: Open a file and read it or copy it to another directory
W	Write	Directory level: Change contents of files in directory File level: Change contents of file
C	Create	Directory level: Create files and subdirectories File level: Salvage deleted files; create and write a file
E	Erase	Directory level: Delete empty directories File level: Delete the file
M	Modify	Directory level: Change directory attributes; re name subdirectories and files File level: Change the file's attributes; rename the file
F	File Scan	Directory level: See files and subdirectories File level: See the file
A	Access Control	Assign security for directory or file

See Your Account Balance (SYSCON)

Include if

- Accounting is installed on the file server

- You have established an account balance for the user

Your account balance determines the amount of network resources available to you. If there is a limit and you go below it, you will be locked out of the system.

Action	Display
1. Access SYSCON.	"Available Topics" menu
2. Choose "User Information."	"User Names" list
3. Choose your name.	"User Information" menu
4. Choose "Account Balance."	"Account Balance" display

Sample "Account Balance" display:

Account Balance For User CHRIS	
Account Balance:	10000
Allow Unlimited Credit:	No
Low Balance Limit:	50

See Your Account Restrictions (SYSCON)

Include if

- You have established account restrictions for the user (even if you don't show users how to see their account restrictions, you should tell them what their restrictions are and what they mean).

Account restrictions affect your ability to log in and control how you work with your password.

Action	**Display**
1. Access SYSCON.	"Available Topics" menu
2. Choose "User Information."	"User Names" list
3. Choose your name.	"User Information" menu
4. Choose "Account Restrictions."	"Account Restrictions" display

Sample "Account Restrictions" display:

```
┌─────────────────────────────────────────────────────┐
│                                                       │
│       Account Restrictions For User YOURNAME          │
│                                                       │
├───────────────────────────────────────────────────── │
│  Account Disabled:                    No              │
│  Account Has Expiration Date:         No              │
│        Date Account Expires:                          │
│  Limit Concurrent Connections:        No              │
│        Maximum Connections:                           │
│  Allow User To Change Password:       Yes             │
│  Require Password:                    Yes             │
│        Minimum Password Length:       5               │
│  Force Periodic Password Changes:     Yes             │
│        Days Between Forced Changes:   40              │
│        Date Password Expires:         June 21, 1990   │
│        Limit Grace Logins:            Yes             │
│            Grace Logins Allowed:      6               │
│            Remaining Grace Logins:    6               │
│            Require Unique Passwords:  No              │
└───────────────────────────────────────────────────────┘
```

Field	Meaning
Account Disabled	If your account is disabled, you cannot log in.
Account Has Expiration Date	Whether there is a date after which you can no longer log in.
Date Account Expires	The date after which you can no longer log in.
Limit Concurrent Connections	Whether the number of workstations you can be logged into at the same time is limited.
Maximum Connections	How many workstations you can be logged on from at the same time.
Allow User to Change Password	Whether you can change your own password.
Require Password	Whether passwords are required on your system.
Miminum Password Length	Minimum number of characters that your password must be.
Force Periodic Password Changes	Whether you are required to change your password periodically.
Days Between Forced Changes	How often you must change your password.

Date Password Expires

The date when you must change your password next.

Limit Grace Logins

Whether you can log in after your old password has expired.

Grace Logins Allowed

How many times you can log in after your old password has expired.

Remaining Grace Logins

How many grace logins you have left.

Require Unique Passwords

Whether you can use a password more than once.

Change Your Password (SYSCON)

All users need to change their passwords. The only reasons not to include this command are if

- You are one of very few installations that don't require passwords

- You force periodic password changes and are certain that users will only change their passwords then

Here's how to change your password when it's not a forced change.

Action	Display
1. Access SYSCON.	"Available Topics" menu
2. Choose "User Information."	"User Names" list
3. Choose your name.	"User Information" menu
4. Choose "Change Password."	"Enter Old Password" prompt
5. Type your old password and press ENTER.	"Enter New Password" prompt
6. Type your new password and press ENTER.	"Retype New Password" prompt
7. Re-type your new password and press ENTER.	Return to "User Information" menu.

See Your Full Name (SYSCON)

The ability to give a user a full name is meant mainly as a tool for supervisors (you can look up a user's full name if you need to jog your memory). The average user will have little need to do this.

Action	Display
1. Access SYSCON.	"Available Topics" menu
2. Choose "User Information."	"User Names" list
3. Choose your name.	"User Information" menu
4. Choose "Full Name."	Full name shown

See the Groups You Belong To (SYSCON)

Include only if user

- Understands NetWare security well enough to know that membership in a group gives them the same trustee rights as that group has.

- Looks at his or her own security (if users look at their own security, it's important for them to know what groups they belong to, because many of their trustee assignments may be given to them via their group membership.)

Most users won't need to know their group membership.

Action	Display
1. Access SYSCON.	"Available Topics" menu
2. Choose "User Information."	"User Names" list
3. Choose your name.	"User Information" menu
4. Choose "Groups Belonged To."	"Groups Belonged To" list

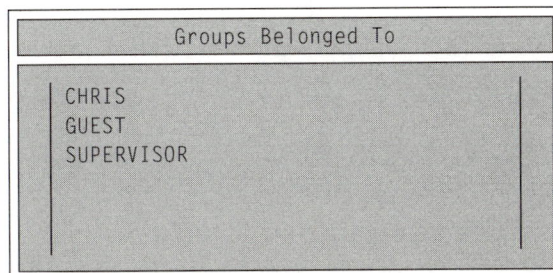

```
             Groups Belonged To
   ┌─────────────────────────────────────┐
   │ CHRIS                               │
   │ GUEST                               │
   │ SUPERVISOR                          │
   │                                     │
   │                                     │
   └─────────────────────────────────────┘
```

See Your Managed Users and Groups (SYSCON)

Include if

- You have implemented the workgroup manager feature

- You have assigned the user to manage other users and groups

Managed users and groups are those that you have been given administrative responsibility for.

Action	Display
1. Access SYSCON.	"Available Topics" menu
2. Choose "User Information."	"User Names" list
3. Choose your name.	"User Information" menu
4. Choose "Managed Users and Groups."	"Managed Users and Groups" list

See a User's Managers (SYSCON)

Include if

- You have implemented the workgroup manager feature

- You have assigned a manager or managers for the user

Your manager is another user or group who has been given administrative responsibility for you.

Action	Display
1. Access SYSCON.	"Available Topics" menu
2. Choose "User Information."	"User Names" list
3. Choose your name.	"User Information" menu
4. Choose "Managers."	"Managers" list

See Security Equivalences (SYSCON)

Include if user

• Knows about NetWare security (only users with a very thorough understanding of NetWare security—including security rights, effective rights,
trustee rights, and inherited rights masks—would ever check their security
equivalences. In addition, users would have to understand that security
equivalences give them the same rights as those that the users or groups
they're equivalent to have directly.)

If you are security-equivalent to a user or group, you have the same security
privileges as that user or group.

Action	Display
1. Access SYSCON.	"Available Topics" menu
2. Choose "User Information."	"User Names" list
3. Choose your name.	"User Information" menu
4. Choose "Security Equivalences."	"Security Equivalences" list

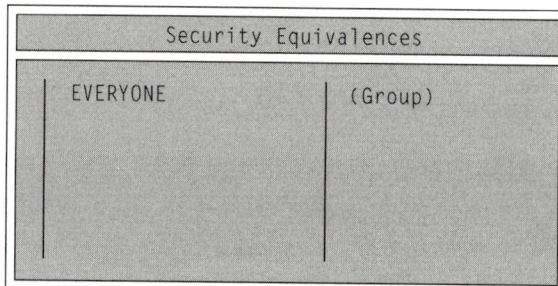

```
┌─────────────────────────────────────────────┐
│           Security Equivalences              │
├──────────────────────┬──────────────────────┤
│ EVERYONE             │ (Group)              │
│                      │                      │
│                      │                      │
│                      │                      │
│                      │                      │
│                      │                      │
└──────────────────────┴──────────────────────┘
```

See Station Restrictions (SYSCON)

Include if user

- Has station restrictions (even then, this information may not be useful, because it is presented in a technical format that is obscure for most users—hexadecimal station addresses, not English-language descriptions).

These are the workstations you can log in from.

Action	Display
1. Access SYSCON.	"Available Topics" menu
2. Choose "User Information."	"User Names" list
3. Choose your name.	"User Information" menu
4. Choose "Station Restrictions."	"Allowed Login Addresses" list

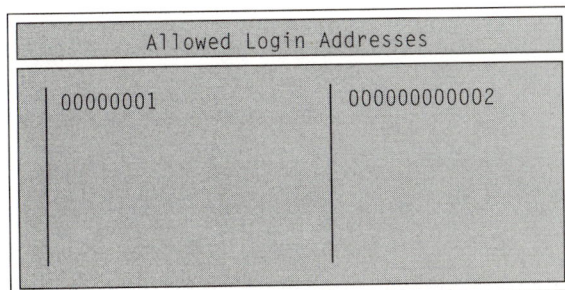

```
          Allowed Login Addresses
     00000001              000000000002
```

See Time Restrictions (SYSCON)

Include if user

- Has time restrictions.

These are the times you can use the network during.

Action	Display
1. Access SYSCON.	"Available Topics" menu
2. Choose "User Information."	"User Names" list
3. Choose your name.	"User Information" menu
4. Choose "Time Restrictions."	See next page

```
              Allowed Login Times For User USERNAME

                        AM                        PM
         1                         1 1 1                     1 1
         2 1 2 3 4 5 6 7 8 9 0 1 2 1 2 3 4 5 6 7 8 9 0 1

Sunday      ***********************************************
Monday      ***********************************************
Tuesday     ***********************************************
Wednesday   ***********************************************
Thursday    ***********************************************
Friday      ***********************************************
Saturday    ***********************************************

                              Sunday 12:00 am To 12:30 am
```

The time periods marked by asterisks are the times that you can use the network; the time periods that are not marked by asterisks indicate the times during which you cannot use the network.

See Your Trustee Directory Assignments (SYSCON)

Include if user

- Knows about NetWare security (most users would check their trustee assignments when troubleshooting to figure out how their effective rights were determined. Only users with a very thorough understanding of NetWare security—including security rights, effective rights, trustee rights, and inherited rights masks—would ever do this.)

These are the directories where you have been given direct security privileges.

Action	Display
1. Access SYSCON.	"Available Topics" menu
2. Choose "User Information."	"User Names" list
3. Choose your name.	"User Information" menu
4. Choose "Trustee Directory Assignments"	"Trustee Directory Assignments"

Sample "Trustee Directory Assignments" screen:

```
              Trustee Directory Assignments

  SYS:\                              [ RWCEMFA]
  SYS:HOME                           [      F ]
  SYS:HOME/CHRIS                     [ RWCEMFA]
  SYS:MAIL/1A000004                  [ RWCEMF ]
  SYS:PLAY                           [ RWCEM A]
```

A brief explanation of the NetWare security rights is contained in the following table. You may wish to include it here for users' convenience.

Here's a brief explanation of the NetWare security rights.

Letter	Right	Lets you ...
S	Supervisory	Exercise all rights for directory or file
R	Read	Directory level: Open a directory's files and read them or copy them to other directories File level: Open a file and read it or copy it to another directory
W	Write	Directory level: Change contents of files in directory File level: Change contents of file
C	Create	Directory level: Create files and subdirectories File level: Salvage deleted files; create and write a file
E	Erase	Directory level: Delete empty directories File level: Delete the file
M	Modify	Directory level: Change directory attributes; re-name subdirectories and files File level: Change the file's attributes; rename the file
F	File Scan	Directory level: See files and subdirectories File level: See the file
A	Access Control	Assign security for directory or file

See Your Trustee File Assignments (SYSCON)

Include if user

- Knows about NetWare security (most users would check their trustee assignments when troubleshooting to figure out how their effective rights were determined. Only users with a very thorough understanding of NetWare security—including security rights, effective rights, trustee rights, and inherited rights masks—would ever do this.)

These are the files where you have been given direct security privileges.

Action   **Display**

1. Access SYSCON.   "Available Topics" menu

2. Choose "User Information."   "User Names" list

3. Choose your name.   "User Information" menu

4. Choose "Trustee File Assignments"   "Trustee File Assignments" shown

See Volume Restrictions (SYSCON)

Include only if you have limited the amount of volume space available to the user.

Action	Display
1. Access SYSCON.	"Available Topics" menu
2. Choose "User Information."	"User Names" list
3. Choose your name.	"User Information" menu
4. Choose "Volume Restrictions."	"Select A Volume" menu
5. Choose the appropriate volume (if necessary).	"User Disk Volume Restrictions"

```
            User Disk Volume Restrictions

    Limit Volume Space?                     No
    Volume Space Limit:                     KBytes
    Volume Space In Use:                  0 KBytes
```

Instructions for Final Formatting

This chapter provides directions for cleaning up and condensing the 386 manuals that you have just created to suit your users' needs. It begins with instructions for WordPerfect users and continues with instructions for users working in other formats, beginning on page 381.

CHAPTER 8

Instructions for Final Formatting

Formatting WordPerfect Files

To do the final formatting of Manual Maker files created in WordPerfect, complete these steps. (Note that keystrokes are contained in brackets or in indented lists.)

1. Retrieve all the files into one file.

    Unless your manuals will be very long (100+ pages), I recommend that you make them all one big file. This will make final formatting easier.

    To retrieve into one file,

    A. Retrieve the first file you wish to include in your manual [SHIFT + F10].

    B. Save the file under a new name—preferably one which describes the manual you're making.

    C. Go to the very end of the file [HOME, HOME, down arrow key].

    D. Retrieve the second file into this file [SHIFT + F10, Yes].

    E. Continue with steps C and D until you have retrieved all the desired files into your manual file. Then save the file again.

2. Turn the Comments display off and fix the spacing.

As noted in the introduction, the Comments contained throughout the text sometimes create some awkward spacing. You may also have created awkward page breaks, very short pages, lines of "orphan" text, etc., as you modified the chapters. Now is the time to fix these problems.

A. Go to the very beginning of your text [HOME, HOME, up arrow key].

B. Turn the Comments display off:
> SHIFT + F1
> Option 2 (Display)
> Option 6 (Edit Screen Options)
> Option 2 (Comments Display)
> No
> Press the Escape key three times

With the Comments display off, you can see the pages as they will actually print. Page through the document and adjust the spacing as desired.

3. Make the page numbering sequential.

Once you have fixed the spacing, you are ready to make sure that your pages will be numbered sequentially. To do so, complete these steps.

A. Go to the very beginning of your text [HOME, HOME, up arrow key].

B. If you wish to begin the manual on a page number other than 1, insert a new page number here at the beginning of the text.

> SHIFT + F8
> Option 2, Page

Option 6, Page Numbering
Option 1, New Page Number
Type the number and press Enter
Press the Escape key three times

C. Search for any new page number codes and delete them:

F2
SHIFT + F8
Option 2, Page
Option 6, PgNum
Option 1, New
Escape
Back arrow key (to delete)
Yes (to confirm deletion)

4. Change the footers if desired.

The unmodified Manual Maker files contain a generic footer which labels the pages "Network User's Guide" and places a sequential page number in the outer corner of each page so you can easily copy double-sided pages. If this suits your needs, you needn't change the footers. If you do wish to change the footers, complete these steps.

A. Search for and delete all the old footers.

First, find and delete the footers on the odd pages:

F2
SHIFT + F8

    Option 2, Page
    Option 4, Ftr
    Option 1, Footer A
    Escape
    Back arrow key (to delete)
    Yes (to confirm deletion)

Then find and delete the footers on the even pages:

    F2
    SHIFT + F8
    Option 2, Page
    Option 4, Ftr
    Option 2, Footer B
    Escape
    Back arrow key (to delete)
    Yes (to confirm deletion)

B. Create new footers (these instructions tell you how to create the same footer on every page. If you wish to do something more complex, consult the WordPerfect manual).

    SHIFT + F8
    Option 2, Page
    Option 4, Footers
    Option 1, Footer A
    Option 2, Every Page
    Type the footer
    (for automatic, sequential page numbering, type (Control + B)
    Press F7 twice to exit

5. Generate the table of contents and correct page references.

The Manual Maker files contain the codes necessary to generate a table of contents and correct page references. You can do both in the same operation.

A. Go to the very end of the document (HOME, HOME, down arrow key).

B. Define the table of contents:
   ALT + F5
   Option 5, Define
   Option 1, Define Table of Contents
   Option 1, Number of Levels
   Escape (to exit)

C. Generate the table of contents and page references.

   ALT + F5
   Option 6, Generate
   Yes

   NOTE: If you try to print before generating, you will get this message: "Document may need to be generated. Print anyway?" This is because the current table of contents and page references are inaccurate, since they were generated in the previous version of the document.

D. Move the table of contents to the desired position in the document, taking care not to throw the pagination off (insert a New Page Number code if necessary).

6. Select the appropriate printer if necessary:

   SHIFT + F7
   Select Printer

(specify the printer)
Escape

7. Print hard copy and proofread it to make sure that your manual appears as you wish it to appear. Make any changes that are still necessary.

8. Once you're satisfied, print final hard copy.

9. Make an archive copy of the final manual and store it in a safe place.

10. Xerox as many copies of your manual as you need, bind them as desired, and distribute them to your users.

Formatting Other Types of Files

If you imported the ASCII text included with this book into a word processor or text editor, you will have to do most of your own internal formatting. If you haven't already done this, go ahead and do so now. Then return to this section for general instructions on final formatting.

1. Retrieve all the files into one file.

   Unless your manuals will be very long (100+ pages), I recommend that you make them all one big file. This will make final formatting easier.

To do so,

   A. Retrieve the first file you wish to include in your manual.

   B. Save the file under a new name—preferably one which describes the manual you're making.

   C. Go to the very end of the file.

   D. Retrieve the second file into this file.

   E. Continue with steps C and D until you have retrieved all the desired files into your manual file. Then save the file again.

2. Delete the Notes to Supervisors.

   I recommend that you create a macro to delete the Notes to Supervisors. I can't tell you the specifics, but generally, the macro should consist of these steps:

   Find the words "Comment Begin"
   Go to the beginning of the word "Comment"

Turn a block on
Find the words "Comment End" (thus marking the block which is the
entire note)
Delete the block

3. Page through the document and adjust the spacing as desired, eliminating any awkward page breaks, etc.

4. Make sure that the page numbering will be sequential.

5. Create footers if desired.

6. Mark the text for a table of contents and index if desired.

7. Print hard copy and proofread it to make sure that your manual appears as you wish it to appear. Make any changes that are still necessary.

8. Once you're satisfied, print final hard copy.

9. Make an archive copy of the final manual and store it in a safe place.

10. Xerox as many copies of your manual as you need, bind them as desired, and distribute them to your users.

Index

A Library of Technical References from M&T Books

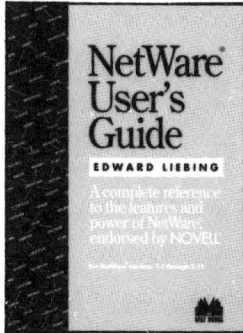

NetWare User's Guide
by Edward Liebing

Endorsed by Novell, this book informs NetWare users of the services and utilities available, and how to effectively put them to use. Contained is a complete task-oriented reference that introduces users to NetWare and guides them through the basics of NetWare menu-driven utilities and command line utilities. Each utility is illustrated, thus providing a visual frame of reference. You will find general information about the utilities, then specific procedures to perform the task in mind. Utilities discussed include NetWare v2.1 through v2.15. For advanced users, a workstation troubleshooting section is included, describing the errors that occur. Two appendixes, describing briefly the services available in each NetWare menu or command line utility are also included.

Book only   **Item #071-0**   **$24.95**

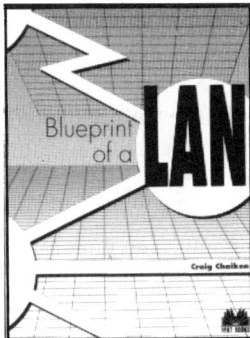

Blueprint of a LAN
by Craig Chaiken

Blueprint of a LAN provides a hands-on introduction to microcomputer networks. For programmers, numerous valuable programming techniques are detailed. Network administrators will learn how to build and install LAN communication cables, configure and troubleshoot network hardware and software, and provide continuing support to users. Included are a very inexpensive zero-slot, star topology network, remote printer and file sharing, remote command execution, electronic mail, parallel processing support, high-level language support, and more. Also contained is the complete Intel 8086 assembly language source code that will help you build an inexpensive to install, local area network. An optional disk containing all source code is available.

Book & Disk (MS-DOS)   **Item #066-4**   **$39.95**

Book only   **Item #052-4**   **$29.95**

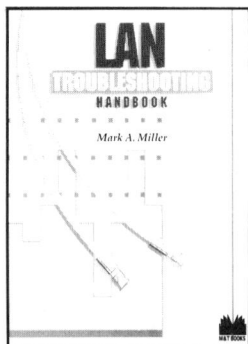

LAN Troubleshooting Handbook
by Mark A. Miller

This book is specifically for users and administrators who need to identify problems and maintain a LAN that is already installed. Topics include LAN standards, the OSI model, network documentation, LAN test equipment, cable system testing, and more. Addressed are specific issues associated with troubleshooting the four most popular LAN architectures: ARCNET, Token Ring, Ethernet, and StarLAN. Each are closely examined to pinpoint the problems unique to its design and the hardware. Handy checklists to assist in solving each architecture's unique network difficulties are also included.

Book & Disk (MS-DOS)	Item #056-7	$39.95
Book only	Item #054-0	$29.95

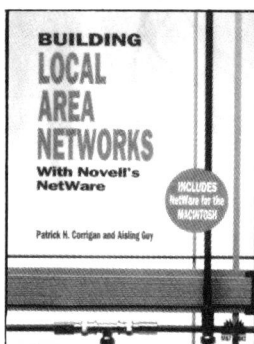

Building Local Area Networks with Novell's NetWare
by Patrick H. Corrigan and Aisling Guy

From the basic components to complete network installation, here is the practical guide that PC system integrators will need to build and implement PC LANs in this rapidly growing market. The specifics of building and maintaining PC LANs, including hardware configurations, software development, cabling, selection criteria, installation, and on-going management are described in a clear "how-to" manner with numerous illustrations and sample LAN management forms. *Building Local Area Networks* gives particular emphasis to Novell's NetWare, Version 2.1. Additional topics covered include the OS/2 LAN manager, Tops, Banyan VINES, internetworking, host computer gateways, and multisystem networks that link PCs, Apples, and mainframes.

Book & Disk (MS-DOS)	Item #025-7	$39.95
Book only	Item #010-9	$29.95

1-800-533-4372 (in CA 1-800-356-2002)

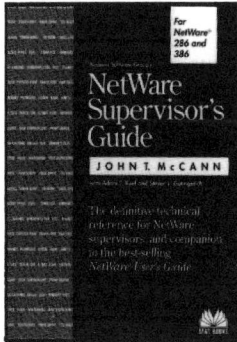

NetWare Supervisor's Guide
by John T. McCann, Adam T. Ruef, and Steven L. Guengerich

Written for network administrators, consultants, installers, and power users of all versions of NetWare, including NetWare 386. Where other books provide information on using NetWare at a workstation level, this definitive reference focuses on how to administer NetWare. Contained are numerous examples which include understanding and using NetWare's undocumented commands and utilities, implementing system fault tolerant LANs, refining installation parameters to improve network performance, and more.

Book only   **Item #111-3**   **$24.95**

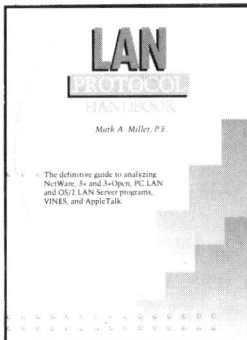

LAN Protocol Handbook
by Mark A. Miller, P.E.

Requisite reading for all network administrators and software developers needing in-depth knowledge of the internal protocols of the most popular network software. It illustrates the techniques of protocol analysis—the step-by-step process of unraveling LAN software failures. Detailed are how Ethernet, IEEE 802.3, IEEE 802.5, and ARCNET networks transmit frames of information between workstations. From that foundation, it presents LAN performnce measurements, protocol analysis methods, and protocol analyzer products. Individual chapters thoroughly discuss Novell's NetWare, 3Com's 3+ and 3+Open, IBM Token-Ring related protocols, and more!

Book only   **Item 099-0**   **$34.95**

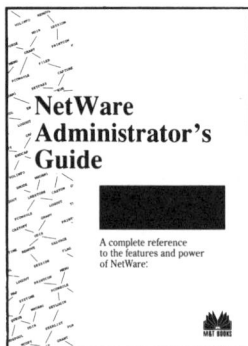

NetWare Administrator's Guide
by Russell Frye

This comprehensive guide is for all NetWare administrators responsible for the daily management of a NetWare network. Through in-depth discussions and detailed explanations, administrators will learn how to increase their network's performance and simplify file server management. All utilities available from the console are thoroughly examined. Readers will learn how to link a NetWare network to other networks, set up and manage remote access services, keep track of cabling layouts, monitor network operations, manage shared resources, and much more.

Book only   **Item #125-3**   **$34.95**

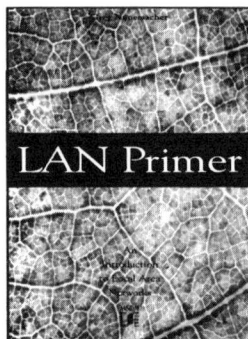

LAN Primer
An Introduction to Local Area Networks
by Greg Nunemacher

A complete introduction to local area networks (LANs), this book is a must for anyone who needs to know basic LAN principles. It includes a complete overview of LANs, clearly defining what a LAN is, the functions of a LAN, and how LANs fit into the field of telecommunications. The author discusses the specifics of building a LAN, including the required hardware and software, an overview of the types of products available, deciding what products to purchase, and assembling the pieces into a working LAN system. LAN Basics also includes case studies that illustrate how LAN principles work. Particular focus is given to ethernet and Token-Ring. Approx. 240 pp.

Book only   **Item #127-X**   **$24.95**

1-800-533-4372 (in CA 1-800-356-2002)

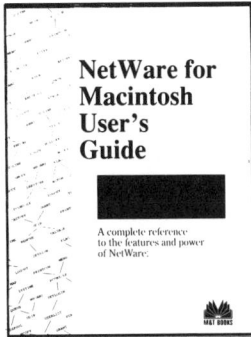

NetWare for Macintosh User's Guide
by Kelley J. P. Lindberg

NetWare for Macintosh User's Guide is the definitive reference to using Novell's NetWare on Macintosh computers. Whether a novice or advanced user, this comprehensive text provides the information readers need to get the most from their NetWare network. It includes an overview of network operations and detailed explanations of all NetWare for Macintosh menu and command line utilities. Detailed tutorials cover such tasks as logging in, working with directories and files, and printing over a network. Advanced users will benefit from the information on managing workstation environments and troubleshooting.

Book only   **Item #126-1**   **$29.95**

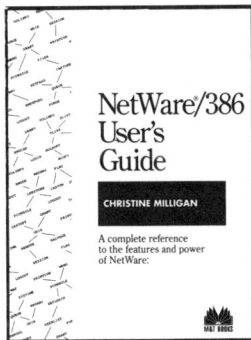

NetWare 386 User's Guide
by Christine Milligan

NetWare 386 User's Guide is a complete guide to using and understanding Novell's NetWare 386. It is an excellent reference for 386. Detailed tutorials cover tasks such as logging in, working with directories and files, and printing over a network. Complete explanations of the basic concepts underlying NetWare 386, along with a summary of the differences between NetWare 286 and 386, are included. Advanced users will benefit from the information on managing workstation environments and the troubleshooting index that fully examines NetWare 386 error messages.

Book only   **Item #101-6**   **$29.95**

NetWare 286 Manual Maker

C H R I S T I N E   M I L L I G A N

The Complete Kit for Creating Customized NetWare 286 Manuals

NetWare 386 Manual Maker

C H R I S T I N E   M I L L I G A N

The Complete Kit for Creating Customized NetWare 386 Manuals

NetWare for Macintosh Manual Maker

The Complete Kit for Creating Customized NetWare Macintosh Manuals

The NetWare Manual Makers
Complete Kits for Creating Customized NetWare Manuals

Developed to meet the tremendous demand for customized manuals, The NetWare Manual Makers enables the NetWare supervisor and administrator to create network training manuals specific to their individual sites. Administrators simply fill in the blanks on the template provided on disk and print the file to create customized manuals and command cards. Included are general "how-to" information on using a network, as well as fill-in-the-blank sections that help administrators explain and document procedures unique to a particular site. The disk files are provided in WordPerfect and ASCII formats. The WordPerfect file creates a manual that looks exactly like the one in the book. The ASCII file can be imported into any desktop publishing or word processing software.

The NetWare 286 Manual Maker
The Complete Kit for Creating Customized NetWare 286 Manuals
by Christine Milligan

Book/Disk   Item #119-9 $49.95

The NetWare 386 Manual Maker
The Complete Kit for Creating Customized NetWare 386 Manuals
by Christine Milligan

Book/Disk   Item #120-2 $49.95

The NetWare for Macintosh Manual Maker
The Complete Kit for Creating Customized NetWare for Macintosh Manuals
by Kelley J. P. Lindberg

Book/Disk   Item #130-X $49.95

1-800-533-4372 (in CA 1-800-356-2002)

Running WordPerfect on NetWare®

Greg McMurdie and
Joni Taylor

Running WordPerfect on Netware
by Greg McMurdie and Joni Taylor

Written by NetWare and WordPerfect experts, the book contains practical information for both system administrators and network WordPerfect users. Administrators will learn how to install, maintain, and troubleshoot WordPerfect on the network. Users will find answers to everyday questions such as how to print over the network, how to handle error messages, and how to use WordPerfect's tutorial on NetWare.

Book only	Item #145-8	$29.95

Graphics Programming in C

A Comprehensive Resource for Every C Programmer

Covers CGA, EGA, and VGA graphic displays and includes a complete toolbox of graphic routines and sample programs

Roger T. Stevens

Graphics Programming in C
by Roger T. Stevens

All the information you need to program graphics in C, including source code, is presented. You'll find complete discussions of ROM BIOS, VGA, EGA, and CGA inherent capabilities; methods of displaying points on a screen; improved, faster algorithms for drawing and filling lines, rectangles, rounded polygons, ovals, circles, and arcs; graphic cursors; and much more! Both Turbo C and Microsoft C are supported.

Book/Disk (MS-DOS)	Item #019-4	$36.95
Book only	Item #018-4	$26.95

Object-Oriented Programming for

PRESENTATION MANAGER

Object-Oriented Programming for Presentation Manager
by William G. Wong

Written for programmers and developers interested in OS/2 Presentation Manager (PM), as well as DOS programmers who are just beginning to explore Object-Oriented Programming and PM. Topics include a thorough overview of Presentation Manager and Object-Oriented Programming, Object-Oriented Programming languages and techniques, developing Presentation Manager applications using C and OOP techniques, and more.

Book/Disk (MS-DOS)	Item #079-6	$39.95
Book only	Item #074-5	$29.95

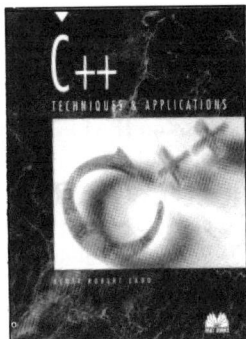

C++ Techniques and Applications
by Scott Robert Ladd

This book guides the professional programmer into the practical use of the C++ programming language—an object-oriented enhancement of the popular C programming language. The book contains three major sections. Part One introduces programmers to the syntax and general usage of C++ features; Part Two covers object-oriented programming goals and techniques; and Part Three focuses on the creation of applications.

Book/Disk (MS-DOS)	Item #076-1	$39.95
Book only	Item #075-3	$29.95

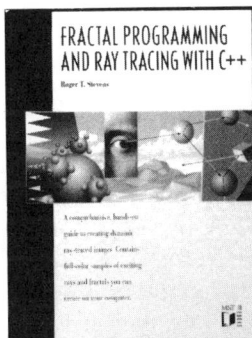

Fractal Programming and Ray Tracing with C++
by Roger T. Stevens

Finally, a book for C and C++ programmers who want to create complex and intriguing graphic designs. By the author of three best-selling graphics books, this new title thoroughly explains ray tracing, discussing how rays are traced, how objects are used to create ray-traced images, and how to create ray tracing programs. A complete ray tracing program, along with all of the source code is included. Contains 16 pages of full-color graphics.

Book/Disk (MS-DOS)	Item 118-0	$39.95
Book only	Item 134-2	$29.95

Advanced Fractal Programming in C
by Roger T. Stevens

Programmers who enjoyed our best-selling *Fractal Programming in C* can move on to the next level of fractal programming with this book. Included are how-to instructions for creating many different types of fractal curves, including source code. Contains 16 pages of full-color fractals. All the source code to generate the fractals is available on an optional disk in MS/PC-DOS format.

Book/Disk (MS-DOS)	Item #097-4	$39.95
Book only	Item #096-6	$29.95

1-800-533-4372 (in CA 1-800-356-2002)

| Advanced Graphics Programming in Turbo Pascal | **Advanced Graphics Programming in Turbo Pascal**
by Roger T. Stevens and Christopher D. Watkins |

Advanced Graphics Programming in Turbo Pascal
by Roger T. Stevens and Christopher D. Watkins

This new book is must reading for Turbo Pascal programmers who want to create impressive graphic designs on IBM PC's and compatibles. There's 16 pages of full color graphic displays along with the source code to create these dramatic pictures. Complete explanations are provided on how to tailor the graphics to suit the programmer's needs. Covered are algorithms for creating complex 2-D shapes including lines, circles and squares; how to create advanced 3-D shapes, wire-frame graphics, and solid images; numerous tips and techniques for varying pixel intensities to give the appearance or roundness to an object; and more.

Roger T. Stevens and
Christopher D. Watkins

Book/Disk (MS-DOS)	Item #132-6	$39.95
Book only	Item #131-8	$29.95

Advanced Graphics Programming in C and C++
by Roger T. Stevens

This book is for all C and C++ programmers who want to create impressive graphic designs on thier IBM PC or compatible. Though in-depth discussions and numerous sample programs, readers will learn how to create advanced 3-D shapes, wire-frame graphics, solid images, and more. All source code is available on disk in MS/PC-DOS format. Contains 16 pages of full color graphics.

Roger T. Stevens

Book/Disk (MS-DOS)	Item #173-3	$39.95
Book only	Item #171-7	$29.95

Graphics Programming with Microsoft C 6.0
by Mark Mallet

Written for all C programmrs, this book explores graphics programming with Microsoft C 6.0, including full coverage of Microsoft C's built-in graphics libraries. Sample programs will help readers learn the techniques needed to create spectacular graphic designs, including 3-D figures, solid images, and more. All source code in book is available on disk in MS/PC-DOS format. Includes 16 pages of full-color graphics.

Mark Mallet

Book/Disk (MS-DOS)	Item #167-9	$39.95
Book only	Item #165-2	$29.95

1-800-533-4372 (in CA 1-800-356-2002)

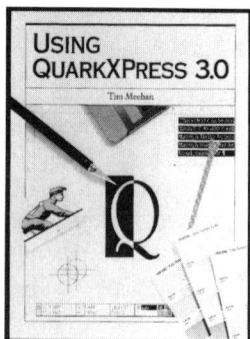

Using QuarkXPress
by Tim Meehan

Written in an enjoyable, easy-to-read style, this book addresses
the needs of both beginning and intermediate users. It includes
numerous illustrations and screen shots that guide readers through
comprehensive explanations of QuarkXPress, its potential and
real-world applications. Using QuarkXPress contains comprehensive explanations of the concepts, practices, and uses of
QuarkXPress with sample assignments of increasing complexity
that give readers actual hands-on experience using the program.

| Book/Disk | Item #129-6 | $34.95 |
| Book only | Item #128-8 | $24.95 |

An OPEN LOOK at UNIX
A Developer's Guide to X
by John David Miller

This is the book that explores the look and feel of the OPEN
LOOK graphical user interface, discussing its basic philiosophy,
environment, and user-interface elements. It includes a detailed
summary of the X Window System, introduces readers to object-
oriented programming, and shows how to develop commercial-
grade X applications. Dozens of OPEN LOOK program examples
are presented, along with nearly 13,000 lines of C code. All
source code is available on disk in 1.2 MB UNIX cpio format.

| Book/Disk | Item #058-3 | $39.95 |
| Book only | Item #057-5 | $29.95 |

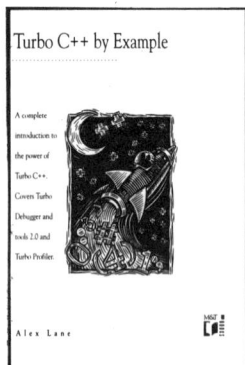

Turbo C++ by Example
by Alex Lane

Turbo C++ by Example includes numerous code examples that
teach C programmers new to C++ how to skillfully program with
Borland's powerful Turbo C++. Detailed are key features of
Turbo C++ with code examples. Includes both Turbo Debugger
and Tools 2.0—a collection of tools used to design and debug
Turbo C++ programs, and Turbo Profiler. All listings available on
disk in MS/PC-DOS format.

| Book/Disk (MS-DOS) | Item #141-5 | $36.95 |
| Book only | Item #123-7 | $26.95 |

1-800-533-4372 (in CA 1-800-356-2002)

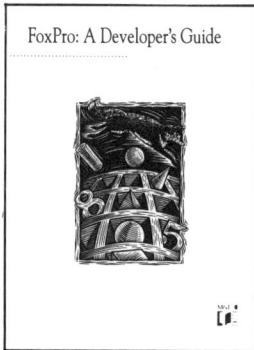

FoxPro: A Developer's Guide
Application Programming Techniques
by Pat Adams and Jordan Powell

Picking up where the FoxPro manual leaves off, this book shows programmers how to master the exceptional power of FoxPro. Useful tips and techniques, along with FoxPro's features, commands, and functions are all covered. Special attention is given to networking issues. Contains discussions on running FoxPro applications on both PCs and Macs that are on the same network. All source code is available on disk in MS/PC-DOS format.

Book/Disk (MS-DOS)	Item #084-2	$39.95
Book only	Item #083-4	$29.95

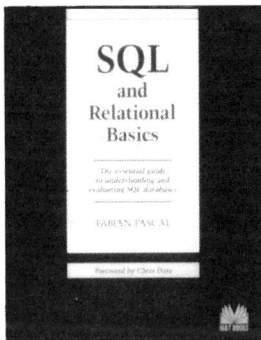

SQL and Relational Basics
by Fabian Pascal

SQL and Relational Basics was written to help PC users apply sound and general objectives to evaluating, selecting, and using database management systems. Misconceptions about relational data management and SQL are addressed and corrected. The book concentrates on the practical objectives of the relational approach as they pertain to the micro environment. Users will be able to design and correctly implement relational databases and applications, and work around product deficiencies to minimize future maintenance.

Book only:	Item #063-X	$28.95

A Small C Compiler, Second Edition
by James Hendrix

This is a solid resource for all programmers who want to learn to program in C. It thoroughly explains Small C's structure, syntax, and features. It succinctly covers the theory of compiler operation and design, discussing Small C's compatibility with C, explaining how to modify the compiler to generate new versions of itself, and more. A full-working Small C compiler, plus all the source code and files are provided on disk in MS/PC-DOS format.

Book/Disk (MS-DOS)	Item #124-5	$29.95

1-800-533-4372 (in CA 1-800-356-2002)

PACKING SLIP
FROM

1838

MILLER & MILLER BOOKSTORE
5151 W. Thunderbird Rd.
Glendale, AZ 85306
602-843-7763

SOLD TO County Attorney, Civil Division

ADDRESS 111 W Monroe, Suite 1600, Px 85003

SHIP TO

ADDRESS

JUL 5 1991 RECEIVED

CUSTOMER'S NO.	SHIPPER'S NO.	SALESMAN	DATE
A 42939			6-28-91

QUANTITY	DESCRIPTION
1	Netware 386 Manual Maker

PACKED BY	CHECKED BY	CARTON-PKGS.	TOTAL WEIGHT	SHIPPED VIA

REDIFORM

6S 639
Poly Pak (50 Sets) 6P639

**PLEASE NOTIFY US IMMEDIATELY
IF ERROR IS FOUND IN SHIPMENT**

O R D E R   F O R M

To Order: Return this form with your payment to M&T books, 501 Galveston Drive, Redwood City, CA 94063 or **call toll-free 1-800-533-4372 (in California, call 1-800-356-2002).**

ITEM #	DESCRIPTION	DISK	PRICE

Subtotal	
CA residents add sales tax ____%	
Add $3.50 per item for shipping and handling	
TOTAL	

Charge my:
- ❏ **Visa**
- ❏ **MasterCard**
- ❏ **AmExpress**

- ❏ **Check enclosed, payable to M&T Books.**

CARD NO. _____

SIGNATURE _____ EXP. DATE _____

NAME _____

ADDRESS _____

CITY _____

STATE _____ ZIP _____

M&T GUARANTEE: If your are not satisfied with your order for any reason, return it to us within 25 days of receipt for a full refund. Note: Refunds on disks apply only when returned with book within guarantee period. Disks damaged in transit or defective will be promptly replaced, but cannot be exchanged for a disk from a different title.

7111

Software License Agreement